WITHDRAWN

JUNE
JORDAN

ffirmative acts

POLITICAL ESSAYS

AFFIRMATIVE ACTS

AFFIRMATIVE ACTS

ACTS

><

Political Essays

><

June Jordan

ANCHOR BOOKS

DOUBLEDAY

New York   London   Toronto   Sydney   Auckland

AN ANCHOR BOOK
PUBLISHED BY DOUBLEDAY
a division of Bantam Doubleday Dell Publishing Group, Inc.
1540 Broadway, New York, New York 10036

ANCHOR BOOKS, DOUBLEDAY, and the portrayal of an anchor are
trademarks of Doubleday, a division of Bantam Doubleday Dell
Publishing Group, Inc.

Some essays were previously published as follows: "Mandela and the Kingdom
Come" (April 1990), "Intifada, USA" (December 1990), "Thomas Was Not
the Point" (November 1991), "The Big-Time Coward" (April 1991), "On the
Night of November 3, 1992" (January 1993), "Valentine's Day" (February
1992), "The Light of the Fire" (June 1992), "Willing and Able" (August
1992), "I Am Seeking an Attitude" (May 1993), "Islam and the USA Today"
(February 1993), "The Truth of Rodney King" (June 1993), "Bosnia Betrayed"
(September 1993), "Freedom Time" (November 1993), "A Good Fight"
(December 1993), "Give Me Two Reasons" (March 1994), "A Powerful
Hatred" (May 1994), "We Are All Refugees" (July 1994), "Innocent of What?"
(September 1994), "Where I Live Now" (January 1995), "Where I Live Now,
Part Two" (March 1995), "In the Land of White Supremacy" (June 1995),
"My Mess, and Ours" (October 1995), "Eyewitness in Lebanon" (August
1996), originally published in *The Progressive*, Madison, Wisconsin. "Root
Canal to the Future of Women" appeared in *Out of the Garden: Women Writers
on the Bible*, C. Büchmann and C. Spiegel, eds. (New York: Fawcett
Columbine), 1994.

Library of Congress Cataloging-in-Publication Data
Jordan, June, 1936–
Affirmative acts / June Jordan.
p.   cm.
1. Afro-Americans—Civil rights.   2. Affirmative action programs—United
States.   3. Afro-Americans—Social conditions—1975–   .
4. Women's rights—United States.   5. Women—United States—Social
conditions.   6. United States—Politics and government—1989–   .
7. United States—Social conditions—1980–   8. Jordan, June, 1936–   .
I. Title.
E185.615.J668   1998
305.896'073—dc21   98-37023
CIP

ISBN 0-385-49225-1

DEDICATED TO

María Poblet

and

all the good stuff

that produced

the revolutionary poem

of her life

and

all the good stuff

the revolutionary poem

of her life inspires

Tanka Para Los Niños

quiero aprender
dime dame sonidos
tus conocidos
libros y lenguas nuestras
estas son las respuestas

maría poblet

In memory of
Dr. Elizabeth Ann Karlin
3/3/44–7/27/98
R.I.P.

I am indebted to Laura Flanders
for the inspiration and the challenge
of all that intelligence
all that love.

I am indebted to Christopher David Meyer:
My best sense of direction
my steady good news
my son.

SPECIAL THANKS TO

E. Ethelbert Miller for all the laughter, all the luggage
Sara Miles for all of her pulling of my coat
Victoria Sanders for all of her painstaking advocacy, counsel, and
   care
Janet Hill for all of her loyalty and vision
Erwin Cho-Woods for all of the grace and the dream

Contents

⊰⊱

AFFIRMATIVE ACTS

MANDELA AND THE

KINGDOM COME

✳

1990

T H E   W O R L D   W A T C H E S for the face of this man. This is
the face hidden and forbidden by force. These are the cheeks and
these are the lips and this is the nose and these are the ears and the
eyes of the head of a country buried in hatred and blood.

It's 5:35 A.M. when I switch on the TV, and somebody's com-
plaining that Mandela's "really late." He'd been scheduled to appear
more than half an hour ago. So he's late. After twenty-seven years in
prison, after seventy-one years of imprisonment inside South African
apartheid, he is not, the reporter complains, on time. What could
possibly explain the delay? Didn't he realize that hundreds of top
international media personnel expected and needed him to show up?
Didn't he understand that this remarkably elite press corps felt very
uncomfortable? It was hot. All morning the sun burned above them
and they could find no shade. There didn't seem to be a cold beer
available for miles.

But suddenly the helicopters rose into the sky. And, like a badly lit, slow-motion movie, you could see a short, pale caravan of cars making its approach to the prison gates. Within minutes, it was happening. He was there. He was here. Hand-in-hand with his comrade and wife, he stood still and he did not smile. And then the two of them began to move: He walked like a man who does not take the earth for granted. He took one step after another with obvious care and delight. Right next to him, Winnie Mandela stayed close, attuned and alert, and radiant.

My spirit divided between terror and tears. Would he be shot? In the American tradition of Dr. King and Malcolm X, was I about to see another Black man felled and bleeding beyond recall?

But this miracle was no kind of rerun! This Nelson Mandela a.k.a. *terrorist* a.k.a. *communist* a.k.a. *felon* who had vowed to resist violence with violence, to acknowledge respect with respect, and to confront the catastrophe of time with total rebellion against the waste and the weakening that time entails, this same Mandela was returning to near-universal tribute and acclaim: "His freedom," a white man on the radio declared, "is the moment the world has been waiting for."

No one would shoot Mandela. He had outlived the usual meanings of mortality. His resolute endurance of hard labor and three decades of solitude and confinement and love suspended and fatherhood snatched away completely mocked the alleged power of only death. You could shoot Mandela but Mandela could not be killed. He would not die. He would not consent to that. We would not consent to that.

He had borne the unimaginable and so he had become the unimaginable among us: A brilliant, steady lover who will neither fawn nor forgive nor forget. This was the man South Africa had hoped to eradicate. This was the life and the dignity that apartheid means to efface. This was the leader that stone and whips and censorship and stone and night after night of no respite and no remnant caress and stone, and the de facto annulment of marriage, the ridicule of desire, the torture of principled conviction, night after night after night of stone and rock and lifting an ax to the rock and smashing the rock for the stone after stone, this was the leader the lover-in-exile that nothing (not even age) could diminish or destroy.

His voice is not deep. His words do not roll and break, mellifluous. He reads from pieces of paper blown by the wind. He hesitates. The page will not turn. He waits. He tries again. The page turns. He goes on.

He is not young. He does not move easily, or fast. He stands tall. His arms rise, effortless, to the clenched fist salute of Black power.

I AM CRYING because I am overwhelmed by victory: The cost is not forgivable. Tears come from someplace uncontrollable and free and right around now anything uncontrollable and everything free looks and feels pretty good to me. I am crying because last week two white men accosted me, calling me "Bitch!" and calling me "Nigger!" and last week Mr. Nelson Mandela was still locked away, a prisoner of racist white men, and I was not sure about the swift and certain demise of apartheid but this morning I am sure. It's over.

His victory is big news. Enemies of his freedom have died or they will die or they must welcome him. This not about the falling apart of the Berlin Wall. This is white Western hegemony acceding to the non-European future of the planet. You cannot rule somebody who would rather die than kneel. You cannot intimidate somebody seeking his freedom or your death.

His victory is big news. This is an African Black man who says, "I stand here before you not as a prophet, but as a humble servant of you, the people." Mandela is not a man of the cloth. The African National Congress is not the Church. Umkhonto we Sizwe, the military wing of the ANC that Mandela founded in 1960, signified and continues to signify armed struggle, here and now, for the kingdom to come, here and now.

He personifies a secular revolt against here and now violations of human rights. He calls on no authority beyond the authority of the pain and the degradation of living in Black South Africa.

Mandela's rhetoric avoids religious or other abstract allusions. He remains specific. He speaks a language appropriate to a task-force committee meeting of actual men and women. He proceeds, meticulous, in his matter-of-fact giving of thanks to "Comrade Oliver Tambo" and to the South African Communist Party and to the South African white women of The Black Sash and to "the mothers and the wives and the sisters" and to his "beloved wife and family" and to "the world community" and he does not, anywhere, thank God.

Mandela bodies forth a humanist, democratic vision in which all human life occupies the first and last position of concern. Human beings create tyrannous conditions: Human beings must overthrow these tyrannies. His practical, pragmatic vocabulary does not accommodate delusion or despair. His summoning forth of "a democratic and free society in which all persons live together in harmony and with equal opportunities" resonates as common sense.

There is a man lifting his daughter high above his own head so that she can see the leader who believes she has the power to be free. There is a young boy climbing the rough hard wall of Cape Town's City Hall. He never looks down and he never looks behind him as he rises high enough to glimpse Mandela just about to address a world that wants to hear whatever he will say. After twenty-seven years of silence imposed by the innermost prisons of South Africa, Mandela chooses this one word from Xhosa, his native language: "*Amandla!*" (Power!)

He hurls the word into the darkness: "Amandla!" (Power!) And the standing throng of 20,000 instantly responds: "*Ngwethu!*" (It is ours!) "*Ngwethu!*" (It is ours!) So be it.

INTIFADA, USA

⊱⊰

1990

THE GIRL LOOKS THIN. She keeps her eyes on the ground. To either side, Israeli soldiers lounge, postmassacre. She is Palestinian. She cannot be more than nine years old. How long will she stay alive? Who is prepared to guarantee another week of her life?

Several days before this photo appeared in the papers here, Israeli soldiers and armed Israeli "settlers" shot and killed twenty men.

They were Palestinians. They had gathered to protest Israeli Prime Minister Yitzhak Shamir's announcement of his government's (completely illegal) plan to build a new settlement (15,000 units) in Arab East Jerusalem. They had gathered to defy the announced intention of Israeli Temple Mount faithful fanatics "to lay a cornerstone" for a new Jewish Temple—in Arab East Jerusalem. They had come out, several thousand unarmed men, to rebuke these latest Israeli violations of pertinent U.N. resolutions, Palestinian territorial rights, and human decency.

As documented by the one existing videotape of the entire episode, Israeli worshippers and soldiers alike had withdrawn absolutely from the danger zone, the stone-throwing zone, *for more than fifteen minutes* before, suddenly, Israeli soldiers and "settlers" reappeared, guns blazing, and fatal. The killers were Israelis. The victims were, all of them, Palestinians. This is not a new equation. This equation is not a tragedy. This is the killer plan fully financed, and otherwise tolerated, by you and me.

Just, for instance, how do you suppose Shamir will pay for the proposed, and completely illegal, new housing in Arab East Jerusalem? The Bush Administration has guaranteed a $400 million loan for these purposes. The Bush Administration, to my knowledge, has not guaranteed a $400 million anything for the homeless or low-income Americans who need shelter, here.

It must be wonderful to live in Israel. Our American taxes give every single Israeli more money, day after day and year after year, more than every single American suffering from cancer or AIDS would ever hope to receive, week after week, from our federal purse. And then there are these bonuses, like $1 billion additional for weapons (because George Bush was maybe going to sell $19 billion worth of weapons to Saudi Arabia) plus, of course, the very very recent $400 million housing deal. And these bonuses arrive on top of $4 billion annual U.S. aid to Israel, a country with barely 3.2 million inhabitants.

And, in case our handouts of money and missiles seem too paltry, Israel expects our unqualified enslavement to something summarily described as a "pro-Israel" position.

Israel continues its military and commercial collaboration with South Africa. Israel refuses international inspection of its nuclear arsenal. Israel refuses to abide by U.N. resolutions that dictate an Israeli exit from the "Occupied Territories"/Palestinian land. Israel expands its illegal "settlements" inside Arab East Jerusalem and the West Bank, the Gaza Strip, the Golan Heights. Israel deports Palestinian nationals. Israel tortures Palestinians, and detains and incarcerates them without trial. Israel closes up Palestinian towns and universities and shuts down Palestinian newspapers, whenever Israel feels like it.

And so, what happens?

Does George Bush rush 250,000 American troops into Jordan, threatening to invade Israel unless Israel relinquishes the "Occupied Territories" that amount to what's left of a homeland for the Palestinian people? Does Bush freeze all loans, aid, and accounts tied to Israel until and unless Israel complies with our Foreign Assistance Act of 1961? (This American law stipulates that no U.S. aid may be provided to countries engaging in a consistent pattern of human-rights abuse.)

No, no, no, no. And why the hell not?

Clearly, a barrel of oil is worth more than any number of Palestinian lives. Clearly, a barrel of oil is worth more than the safety of the 250,000 young African-American and Mexican-American and Latino and poor white men and women now sweltering on the Arabian desert while they await God-knows-what horrible and un-due and untimely death.

I say we need a rising up, an Intifada, USA.

I have been circulating a petition where I live and work, and I hope others will circulate their own and then sponsor rallies, teach-ins, strikes, boycotts, whatever it takes to stand against the Persian Gulf "standoff."

We need to rise up. We need to stand against the "standoff" in the Persian Gulf. We need an Intifada, USA.

AT NIGHT, I go to bed afraid to close my eyes, or sleep: I ask my soul these questions aching on my conscience: What will happen to that little girl, that child of Palestine? What is happening to you and me?

Thomas Was Not

the Point

✠

1991

THE LAW of the land governs all of our disparate lives. Against the chaos of conflict and above the passions of self-interest, the civilizing power of the law depends upon an ethical consensus on the common good. And because we, the diversity of American people, seldom remain the same from one decade to the next, and because our national condition changes with the history of every day, there can be no absolute law nor any ultimate interpretation of the law.

And yet we must have peace. Within our unstable environment, we search for justice—a commonly accepted, lawful means to the settlement of profound dispute and a commonly accepted, lawful means to the nonviolent allocation, and reallocation, of rights.

The Supreme Court presides over these needs of a democratic state. Since each justice enjoys a lifelong appointment to the bench, there is provision for stability. And as each presidential nominee submits to congressional scrutiny, there is provision for reasonably popular and up-to-date input regarding the political and philosophical composition of this highest court. That would seem to be the ideal plan.

But quite a few things tend to go wrong. Too many Presidents have viewed the Court as a dugout for buddies. Too many members of Congress have abdicated their representative functions: Repeatedly they restrict themselves to mock investigation into the personal probity of this or that candidate. Too often, organized citizens have fastened themselves to the task of advocating or assassinating a particular nominee rather than pressuring Congress to resist or to endorse the President, on principle.

This pattern derives, I believe, from a surrender to unhappy precedent, and a misunderstanding of the democratic principle at stake.

As a people, we Americans are becoming more heterogeneous. Those who determine the law of the land must, therefore, embody an increasing diversity of background and conviction or, for example, the highest court will lose its capacity for justice: It will lose its credibility as an agency responsible to and expressive of ethical consensus.

If we cherish rule by law rather than rule by force, then we must oppose the furtherance of a Supreme Court of like-minded colleagues even as the living components of our body politic become less and less homogeneous. Otherwise, there will emerge a dangerous disjuncture between the judges and the judged.

One fact lay embedded in the center of the Clarence Thomas controversy: We have lost a great American jurist, Thurgood Marshall. No one can replace him. The very thought of replacing him insults the brilliance of his career and the exceptional humanity of his intelligence as he reflected upon our most extreme and consequential public debates. And yet someone new had to be appointed to take his seat.

The President made his move. He nominated a man as different from Marshall as George Bush differs from Mahatma Gandhi. He nominated a man whose most striking characteristic seems to be that of satisfied self-hatred, a man whose public condemnation of his sister strikingly revealed his attitude toward the poor and the weak.

For some, the issue became Black manhood or the sentimentalized biography of Clarence Thomas. They focused upon who the candidate was rather than what he has done and will do. This was identity politics taken to its lowest level.

On the American Right, however, there was more clarity. Among those who detested Thurgood Marshall and who generally despise Black men there was a willingness to promote Clarence Thomas because Clarence Thomas was not the point: The point is to homogenize the Supreme Court. If someone with Black skin will serve that purpose, then fine!

But we, the people, must not yield to judgment without representation. If we yield, there will be no justice. And without justice, believe me, there will be no peace.

THE BIG-TIME COWARD

>≡<

1991

ON A RECENT cold Sunday morning in Kennebunkport, Maine, George Bush and his wife, Barbara, seated themselves inside a small country church of God. (To think about what?)

Alma Powell, wife of the chairman of the Joint Chiefs of Staff of the U.S. armed forces, reports that she likes to keep "comforting foods" like vegetable soup ready, on top of the stove, for Colin, her certainly hardworking husband. Alma adds that, these days, she just "knows" that her Colin doesn't want to hear "little stories" about the children.

Secretary of Defense Dick Cheney, second only to his boss in bloodthirst for arm's-length/armchair warfare, has never served half an hour, even, in the army, the navy, the air force, or the marines. (I know; it's not right to pick on him just for that.)

One recent Saturday, at a local antiwar rally organized by the Middle East Children's Alliance, I noted, aloud, that the war, to date, was costing us $56 billion. Every twenty-four hours, the cost was $1 billion, at least. Therefore, I proposed the following to the crowd scattered on the grass and under the trees:

> One billion dollars a day for seven days for Oakland!
> Can you imagine that?
> One billion dollars a day!
> But to hell with imagination!
> This is our city!
> This is our money!
> These are our lives!
> One billion dollars a day for seven days for Oakland!
> (Or) do we accept that there is only 'the will and
> the wallet' when it's about kill or be killed?
> Do we need this money or not?
> Do we need it here?
> Do we need it now?
> And so on.

WHEN I LEFT the stage a reporter came up to me: "You meant one *million* dollars, didn't you?" "No!" I answered him, amazed: "One billion: One billion dollars a day for seven days for Oakland! That's the bill, that's our bill for housing and drug rehabilitation and books in the public schools and hospital care and all of that good stuff: One billion dollars a day.

"It's a modest proposal: In less than three months, those maniacs in the White House and the Pentagon have spent $56 billion in my name and with my taxes, trying to obliterate Iraq and its people and their leader. I'm saying, call home the troops and the bucks! We need these big bucks to make this a homeland, not a desert. Right here, for the troops and for you and for me: What's the problem? It's a bargain! Seven billion dollars on the serious improvement of American life in Oakland versus $56 billion for death and destruction inside Iraq! What's the problem?"

But the reporter was giving me a weak smile of farewell that let me understand he found my proposal preposterous: One *million* dollars for life, okay. Billions for kill or be killed, okay. But really big bucks on us, the people of these United States? One billion dollars a day to promote, for example, the safety and educational attainment and communal happiness of 339,000 Americans? I must be kidding!

As I walked away from the park, I felt a heavy depression overtaking me: The reporter, a tall white man with clear eyes, could not contemplate the transfer of his and my aggregate resources from death to life as a reasonable idea. Worse, he could not suppose his and my life to be worth anything close to the value of organized, high-tech, and boastful murder.

But then other people stopped me to ask: "How can we do that? Do we write letters or what?" And so as I write this column tonight, I am reassured because not every American has lost her mind or his soul. Not everyone of my compatriots has become a flag-wrapped lunatic lusting after oil/power/the perversions of "kicking ass," preferably via TV.

A huge number of Americans have joined with enormous numbers of Arab peoples and European communities in Germany, England, France, Italy, Spain, and Muslim communities throughout India and Pakistan to cry out, "Stop!"

And when I say "huge," I mean it: If one thousand Americans contacted by some pollster can be said to represent 250 million people, then how many multi-multi-millions do we, antiwar movement gatherings of more than 100,000, coast to coast and on every continent, how many do we represent?!

And how come nobody ever does that kind of political math?

And tonight, February 22, 1991, when yet again the ruling white men of America despise peace and sneer at negotiations and intensify their arm's-length/armchair prosecution of this evil war, this display of a racist value system that will never allow for any nationalism that is not their own and that will never allow Third World countries to control their own natural resources and that will never express, let alone feel, regret or remorse or shame or horror at the loss of any human life that is not white, tonight I am particularly proud to be an African-American.

• • •

BY AUTHORIZING the heaviest air assault in history against Iraq on January 15, 1991, George Bush dared to desecrate the birthday of Martin Luther King, Jr. Tonight, 83,000 bombing missions later, is the twenty-sixth anniversary of the assassination of Malcolm X.

On this sorry evening the world has seen the pathological real deal behind the sanctimonious rhetoric of Bush and Company: The Persian Gulf War is not about Iraqi withdrawal from Kuwait. The war is not about Kuwait at all. Clearly it's not about international law or respect for United Nations resolutions since, by comparison to Washington, Tel Aviv, and Pretoria, "the Butcher of Baghdad" is a minor-league Johnny-come-lately to the realm of outlaw conduct and contempt for world opinion.

What has happened tonight is that the Soviet leader, Mikhail Gorbachev, and the government of Iraq have reached an agreement whereby Iraq would withdraw from Kuwait, and that is a fact—regardless of anything else included or omitted by the proposal. This agreement should provide for an immediate cease-fire, a cessation of the slaughter of Iraqi men and women, and a halt to the demolition, nationwide, of their water supply, their access to food, their securement of shelter.

So what is the response of the Number One White Man in America? He's gone off "to the theater." I guess that means the nearest church was closed. Or that Colin Powell was busy dipping his spoon into the comfort of a pot of soup somebody else cooked for him. And that Dick Cheney was fit to be tied into any kind of uniform so long as it meant nobody would take away his Patriot missiles and Apache helicopters and B-52 cluster-bomb bombers and Black and brown and poor white soldiers and sailors and all the rest of these toys for a truly big-time coward.

Confronted with the "nightmare" prospect of peace, Bush goes off to the theater because he'll be damned if he will acknowledge that Saddam Hussein is a man, is the head of a sovereign state, is an enemy to be reckoned with, an opponent with whom one must negotiate: Saddam Hussein is not a white man! He and his Arab peoples must be destroyed! No peace! No cease-fire! No negotiations!

And I am proud tonight to remember Dr. King and Malcolm X, and to mourn their absence, even as I pursue the difficult challenge of their legacy. Both of these men became the targets of white wrath when they, in their different ways, developed into global visionaries persisting against racism in Alabama, in Harlem, in South Africa, in Vietnam. Neither of these men could have failed to condemn this current attack against the Arab world. Neither of these men ever condoned anything less than equal justice and equal rights. Hence, the undeniably racist double standards now levied against Saddam Hussein would have appalled and alienated both of them, completely.

I am proud to shake hands with the increasing numbers of African-American conscientious objectors.

I am proud to remark the steadfast moral certainty of Representative Ronald Dellums's opposition to this war.

I am proud to hear about the conscientious objections of Representatives Gus Savage and John Conyers and Mervyn Dymally.

I am proud to observe that, even while African-Americans remain disproportionately represented in the U.S. armed forces, we, as a national community, stand apart from all vagaries of popular opinion; we maintain a proportionately higher-than-white level of opposition to this horrible war, this horrendous evasion of domestic degeneration and decay.

And I want to say something else, specifically to you, Mr. President: It's true you can humiliate and you can hound and you can smash and burn and terrify and smirk and boast and defame and demonize and dismiss and incinerate and starve and, yes, you can force a people to surrender what remains of their bloody bowels into your grasping, bony, dry hands.

But all of us who are weak, we watch you. And we learn from your hatred. And we do not forget. And we are many, Mr. President.

We are most of the people on this godforsaken planet.

ON THE NIGHT OF

NOVEMBER 3, 1992

>€

THERE WAS GREAT rejoicing all over the land. George Bush was out. And inside my little house, the mood fluctuated between stunned reverence and invincible joy.

Moving easily among the nonfat, noncholesterol chocolate-chip cookies, or cakes, and three flavors of frozen yogurt, my friends finished off their champagne and started up (decaffeinated) coffee and I could not remember feeling so much at home before; so safe!

My friends looked like big America writ small in loving needlepoint: African-American men and women and Chinese- and Vietnamese- and Irish- and English- and French-Americans and one Black teenager and one white child and Jewish and gentile and heterosexual and gay and lesbian and married and single and Southern and East Coast and Middle Western and nine years old to fifty-six, and nobody fighting and nobody bitter and nobody mad.

In the justified euphoria of that American moment, it was easy to let go of the horror and dread and shame of the last twelve years. Everything good and necessary seemed possible.

We could fathom and then destroy the reasons for the righteous fires of the Los Angeles revolt.

We could memorialize and never again countenance anything like the Salem, Oregon, hate-crime incineration of Hattie Cohens, a twenty-nine-year-old Black lesbian, and her white, gay housemate, forty-five-year-old Brian Mock.

We could do away with the stupidity of the so-called "politically correct" debate and, instead, undertake the creation of a new American core education worthy of the old and the emerging majorities of Americans who already fill or drop out of our public schools.

We could properly fund and enshrine our public libraries as the open doors to accurate, multicultural, multiracial, multiethnic, multilingual information that they must become.

We could terminate the awful absurdity of a national argument about who controls a woman's body and her mind.

We could make terrific Grade-A PG family-value movies about the hero and the heroine doctors who perform abortions and who provide contraceptive advice despite death threats and bully picket lines and blown-up clinics.

We could cure AIDS.

We could cure breast cancer.

We could learn to praise and lavishly remunerate the nurses and the neighborhood volunteers who comfort and who feed the victims of these killer afflictions.

We could halt and forever forswear the demonization of Arabs and of everybody else who may very well hold different, "un-American" ideas about how things should be in a "new world order."

We could invest the cost of three or four B-2 bombers into the complete, redemptive, *onsite-resident-rebuilding* of our inner cities.

We could do this. It could happen. We were here to testify. As a people, we had spoken and we had won!

But now it was growing late. And one of my friends, Adrienne, sat down at the piano and began to play. And then another of my friends, André, joined her in a love song he'd written years ago—

"There may come a time when hunger's not known/and we'll stop the abuse of the Earth, our home. . . ." And then Adrienne modulated from that R&B ballad mode into a gospel takeover of the keyboard and suddenly André was singing, "O beautiful for spacious skies, for amber waves of grain/for purple mountain majesties above the fruited plain. . . ." I looked over my shoulder and I could see André's son, seventeen-year-old Mike, standing, loose, and listening to his father, and checking out the gorgeous, daring trust that underlay the whole impromptu delivery of the music:

". . . and crown thy good with brotherhood . . ."

And I was thinking, "Bet: Bill Clinton doesn't know the half of what all his energetic rhetoric about change and hope has started up and set ablaze!"

ANDRÉ IS a Black man in his thirties. He works full-time at one job, and part-time at another regular job as well. Three years ago, he abandoned his career as an R&B singer/songwriter/performer to become the full-time single parent of his only child, Mike. In fact, André rescued his son from an abusive home situation and has dedicated himself to activist parenting of a teenager who, among other things, is homophobic.

André is gay. His son, Mike, is not. André sings and writes R&B ballads. Mike writes rap. And I had been getting to know him and some of his ideas about rap when the Simi Valley verdict of "not guilty" exploded everything. This happened close to the end of Mike's last semester in high school, so he just decided to quit, because "school was messed up, too. They had lost my transcript. And I did my homework but the teacher said I didn't . . . so I left. It was like a burden off my shoulders, really.

"And that same week of the Rodney King thing and this man broke into the lady's house right downstairs from us. And all of a sudden there was this pounding on the door and the lady said what was going on. So I picked up a stick and I went downstairs and I went outside and I was looking for the robber a little bit. Then the police come and they rush up and they grab me. They throw me to the ground: A Black lady and a Chinese man. And they ask me for identification. But I never carry no ID. So I said, "Well, I live here!" And they ask me to prove it! And they still trying to lock me up and the Black lady police she put handcuffs on me and push my face in the concrete, and man that hurted me, too, and she stuck her leg in my back. And around that time my dad look out the window and he come down and talk to the police and I was hellified mad but André tell me to go inside and he stay out there and talk to the police, I guess."

Not long after this, Mike split from his father's house. And André searched and walked the streets, but could not find him. Mike had disappeared. And André lived crazy with fear: Where was his boy? Who would listen to him? ("Well, I live here!") Who or what would bring him back alive?

After a couple of months, Mike came home. Maybe he thought that the deal that André offered him—a home and financial support as long as he stays in school—was as good a deal as anything out here, or better. Maybe he just missed his father and their ongoing arguments about most of the things teenagers fight with their parents about. Maybe he thinks André has the best damned family values he ever heard of.

Whatever the reason, Mike was back. And his eyes were soft as he stood, listening to the song about America.

And when I asked Mike how he felt about the Clinton victory, did he feel hopeful, he said, "Kinda. Sort of." And then he let me hear snatches from a rap he'd recently stopped working on:

Now I'm not really a political rapper
But this new shit is just as fishy as a snapper
1992 the year of correction
the out-with-the-old-in-with-the-new election

Will he clean up health care
wipe out welfare?
All I really wanna know

what's he gonna do for me
stop the drug problem; clean
up my community

Constitution after Constitution after Constitution
is broken
It's time to leave the courthouse smokin
Go to the corner store/buy me some gas
C'mon back and throw some flames on that ass
Cause that's the only way/all this madness gone cease
I said it before/No Justice: No peace!

Mike reiterated that he was no longer working on that rap. And maybe he won't bother to finish it. Or maybe he will. But he's back. He's in school. And, on the night of November 3, 1992, he was here, in my house, with his father. And he stood around, drinking Diet Pepsi, and polishing off the food on his plate, and watching the rest of us do instant analysis, and celebrate.

AND WHEN his father's soul baritone merged with Adrienne's gospel rendition of that prayer about our "spacious skies," Mike did not leave. He did not disappear. He stayed where he was standing, at ease. And he stood there, willing to listen and to see what would happen next.

And I don't know what will happen. But André, Mike's father, has never given up on this country, or his son. And he's working hard. And he plays by the rules.

And looking at him, and looking at Mike, and resting my eyes upon Adrienne and David and Carolyn and George and Ben and Temu and Margaret and Minh-Ha and Jean-Paul and Fran and Daniel and Evelyn and Amy and Roberta and Lauren and Will—all of my friends who came into a happy and diverse American community of our own making—I could almost touch the infinitely deep and delicate hope that a landslide of election results had given birth to.

And because revolution always takes place on the basis of great hope and rising expectations, I am not too worried about the future.

One way or the other, a whole lotta change is gonna come. Through happiness realized or through and beyond the pain of betrayal, we will become the beneficiaries of our faith.

And even without revolution, we will prevail because we have proven to the world, and to ourselves, that we are not "fringe elements" or "special-interest groups" or so-called "minorities." Without us there is no legitimate majority: We are the mainstream. We have become "the people."

And let our elected leadership beware the awesome possible wrath of a mighty, multifoliate, and faithful people whose deepest hopes have been rekindled and whose needs have not been met.

VALENTINE'S DAY, 1992

⊰⊱

IT'S A LITTLE bit hard to focus on lace and flowers in the wake of Clarence Thomas and George Bush. I mean you feel a little bit stupid choosing mellow music, lighting candles, and planning a long hot bubbly bath with somebody wonderful when the head nitwit in charge of the whole show says he was offended by "the filth" and "the indecency" of the televised trials of Patricia Bowman and Senator Kennedy's nephew.

I am offended by the filth and the indecency of rape. It's not television that bothers me: It's the brutality of trial proceedings based on the assumption that women regularly lie about rape because we love all the attention we get when everybody examines our underwear/our diaries/the length of our skirt/the height of our heels/ our attitudes toward sex. For example: Is it or is it not true that you have been known to want and to enjoy sex with somebody you were meeting for the first time (who was, of course, also meeting you for the first time and who also wanted and who also enjoyed sex with you on that same basis)?

Anyway, thanks to Clarence and thanks to George, I am un-equivocal, this year, about what (not who) I want for Valentine's Day: I want power! I want truly enormous political power: I want power proportionate to the needs and proportionate to the numbers of women in these United States. And any leader, any candidate, any platform, any feminist agenda, any women's studies' curriculum that fails to nail itself to the task of empowerment of women contributes to the enemy environment in which we barely stay alive.

For instance, here at the University of California–Berkeley, there's a worsening income disparity between men and women on senior-rank faculty levels, and not even 10 percent of the faculty is female. Nationwide, the gender disparity in income holds firm against us. In the U.S. Senate and the U.S. House of Representatives, you will find not even 10 percent female representation.

And then there's the huge number of families headed by women who, because they are women and because day care is a "woman's issue," must battle against poverty with less and less federal and state aid. (In California, Governor Wilson proposes as much as a 25 per-cent reduction of benefits for already desperate AFDC households.)

And everywhere in America, the number of children subjected to poverty rose from 16 percent to 20.1 percent during the last decade.

And there's the growing assault upon our right to choose whether we will have the children our government refuses to shelter and feed.

And every year the violence of the war against women becomes more harrowing and the statistics become less abstract and the songs rappin' out hatred of women advance to a popular big beat.

And in 1991 the demand for emergency food increased 100 percent in Boston and 70 percent in Philadelphia.

And every single year 175,000 American women learn they have breast cancer. This year alone, 45,000 American women will die of breast cancer. And yet the National Cancer Institute allocates only $90 million for research into this tragedy.

In Brazil, one woman in nine is an AIDS victim.

In Africa, the number of orphans created by AIDS will increase, during the next eight years, to ten to fifteen million, while the number of infants born with the HIV infection will rise from the current 750,000 to four million.

How many women dead from AIDS do these terrible facts imply? This is the ground on which we stand. It's political ground. And if we do not think, bottom line, David Duke—if we do not mobilize to stand our ground against David Duke and his closet competitors in the White House and in the state capitols across the country— then we will not only lose the ground under our feet: We will be buried there.

But let me close with a more traditional Valentine salutation: This is my Valentine to Tom Holt, history professor at the University of Chicago. In October 1991, Holt sent out a letter asking for one thousand Black men to join with him and donate $26.50 each to defray half the cost of a full-page *New York Times* ad composed by "African-American Women in Defense of Ourselves"—against the public humiliation of Anita Hill and the Supreme Court seating of Clarence Thomas. This historic coming together of Black women and Black men was conceived and organized by Barbara Ransby, Ph.D. candidate, University of Michigan, Professor Elsa Barkley Brown, University of Michigan, and Professor Deborah King of Dartmouth College. I send my Valentine greetings to these three women, as well.

I take heart from this altogether happy precedent: We can politicize our strength. Yes! We can learn how to love each other enough to seize and determine the everyday/everynight politics of our beleaguered, wistful lives.

THE LIGHT OF THE FIRE

⋺⋵

1992

FIRE EVERYWHERE! across the miasma of Los Angeles, the flames lift into the night and they proliferate. They rise, explosive, from my heart.

Is there horror? Is there heat unbearable? And is there light where, otherwise, we could not see ourselves? Is there an unexpected, unpredictable colossal energy alive and burning, uncontrolled, throughout America?

Behold my heart of darkness as it quickens now with rage! Behold the hundred—no, a thousand—young Black men whose names you never knew/whose neighborhoods you squeezed into a place of helpless desolation/whose music you despised/whose backward baseball caps and baggy jeans you sneered at/whose mothers you denied assistance/whose fathers you inducted into the army or you broke to alleyways where, crumbling at the marrow of their spine, they aged in bitterness.

Behold them now: revengeful, furious, defiant, and, for hours on end, at least, apparently invincible: They just keep moving, and the fires burn. And white kids and Chicanos and Chicanas join them, yes! And Asian-American teenagers join them, yes! There they stand or run, beside and among these young Black men who will not bow down. They will not say, "OK. I am nobody. I have nothing. And you hate me and that's fine! Where should I sign, now, for service to my country? Show me how to worship at the shrine of law and order."

What happened? How come we finally woke up? Why would a jury's verdict of "Not Guilty" galvanize and rescue so many from protracted, profound passivity, suicidal torpor, and fratricidal craziness? How come all of the steady, punitive, self-righteous, and official attacks on poor people didn't get us going?

How come presidential vetoes of civil-rights legislation and the unspeakable onslaught of Clarence Thomas as replacement for Supreme Court Justice Thurgood Marshall didn't push us into the streets?

How come the *senseless* and racist throwaway of $42 billion on Operation Desert Storm didn't pack the highways with a 3,000-mile-long caravan of fired-up folk determined to evict killer lunatics from the White House and the Pentagon?

How come?

We had seen the eighty-one-second videotape of Los Angeles police attacking Rodney King.

We thought, we believed, that this time, and for once, the cops could not escape. Their brutality was clear. Their brutality was nauseating. The case was opened and would soon be shut. We viewed the trial as a procedural nicety. We would actually live to see one important episode of equality before the law! And then the jury found for the defendants. The jury concluded that there never came a moment when they felt, as they watched four cops attack an unarmed Black man—there never came a moment when they felt "enough is enough."

And get this straight: The jury watched police surround Rodney King. They made him lie down on the street, facedown on the street.

They beat him. They stomped him. They hog-tied his hands and feet. They shot him four times with a Taser gun that injected fifty thousand volts of electricity into his nervous system with each shot.

But that was not too much. That was never excessive force: not for that jury. Not one member of the jury was a Black man or a Black woman. Rodney King was denied due process according to the law. He was not judged by a jury of his peers.

And what was the crime of Rodney King? He was a young Black man, not yet dead, and not yet ready, and not yet willing to die: He was Black. He should have been dead. He should not have been born.

Or, as defense attorneys for the police explained, Rodney King kept getting up on "all fours." He wouldn't stay down. He kept raising up his head. He kept rising and rising. He would not lie down. He never assumed "a compliant mode."

And now we have Los Angeles in flames. The mode is nowhere compliant. People of color run around, or walk, without fear. We're off our knees. Heads up, fists in the air, and fire everywhere.

I CONDEMN and deplore the violence of poverty and the injustice of hatred and the violence of absolute injustice that makes the peaceful conduct of our days impossible or cowardly.

Twelve years ago, when Miami police murdered Arthur McDuffie and Black people rose up, I wrote:

"It was such good news. A whole lot of silence had ended at last! Misbegotten courtesies of behavior were put aside. There were no leaders. There were no meetings, no negotiations. A violated people resisted with violence. An extremity of want, an extremity of neglect . . . had been met, at last, with an appropriate, extreme reaction. . . .

"And why should victims cover for their executioners? Why should the protesters cooperate and agree to discuss or write letters? . . .

"But this has been the code, overwhelmingly for the oppressed: That you keep cool and calm and explore proper channels and above all that you remain law-abiding and orderly precisely because . . .

it is the power of the law of the terrorist state arrayed against you to force you to beg and bleed without acceptable recourse except for dumb endurance or mute perishing. . . .

"If you make and keep my life horrible, then, when I can tell the truth, it will be a horrible truth, it will not sound good or look good, or God willing, feel good to you, either. . . ."

Twelve years later and I understand that anarchy is not about nice. I understand that the provocation for anarchy is always and ever the destruction of every reasonable basis for hope. And tonight I know that the Simi Valley, California, jury's verdict of "Not Guilty" feels like the destruction of any reason for hope.

But I must conclude that "the good news" of the 1980 Miami uprising was politically indefensible as such because it did not lead to something big, new, humane, and irreversible. Today, for example, there is another victim of state violence: Rodney King.

And I believe we must take care not to become like our enemies: I do not accept that we should fall upon a stranger, outnumber him or her, and beat and possibly kill our "prey."

And I believe we must take care to distinguish between our enemies and our allies, and not confuse them or forget the difference between a maniac and a potential comrade.

And I have learned about the histories of Native Americans and Chicanos and Asian-Americans and progressive white peoples in these United States and I know that we have more in common than our genuine enemies want us to realize.

And on this evening of the first day after the jury's "Not Guilty" verdict, I attended and I spoke at a rally across from the Superior Court Building, here in Oakland. And the five hundred–plus Americans gathered there embodied the full racial and ethnic and class and age and sexual diversity that will give us the political and moral strength that we need for successful revolution.

And, as the graffiti proclaimed on the lone wall still standing after flames gutted an L.A. bank, LA REVOLUCIÓN ES LA SOLUCIÓN.

THIS ENORMOUS MOMENT belongs only to each of us. Now we can choose to free ourselves from cross-cultural ignorance and secondhand racist divisions of thought and response. We can unite in our demands for equal human rights and civil liberties.

We can secure further prosecution of lawless police in L.A. We can change the nature of official power. We can gain a second Bill of Rights that will deliver at least as much money to support every African-American child as we spend on the persecution and imprisonment of young Black men.

I am talking just for starters. Obviously, a second Bill of Rights should, and would, bring new entitlements into the life of every kind of American citizen. But these necessary, humane, irreversible, and democratic gains cannot be won without political and moral unity centered on principle rather than identity.

And I am writing tonight by the light of the fire everywhere. The begging body grows cold.

I am beginning to smell something clean. I am beginning to sense a victory of spirit risen from the death of self-hatred. I am beginning to envision our collective turning to the long-term tasks of justice and equal rights to life, liberty, and the pursuit of happiness right inside this country that has betrayed our trust repeatedly. Behold the fire everywhere!

WILLING AND ABLE

⋙⋘

1992

LAST JUNE, Charlie Lubin graduated from Berkeley High School. Three days a week you can catch him at work in the cafeteria of his alma mater. Other times he's busy at a local silkscreen shop, producing T-shirts to order. Or he's out playing softball, or he's studying to become a clown.

Charlie Lubin is twenty-two years old. He was born with Down's syndrome. Right after his birth, hospital doctors and nurses counseled his mother with these words: "Don't see it!"

But Barbara Lubin refused to surrender her child into those waiting, professional hands of death. "That crazy woman with a retarded son" fought to keep him alive, and she kept fighting all the way to *Lubin v. Berkeley Board of Education,* a 1978 landmark legal battle that established the rights of disabled children to an appropriate, and fully conceived and fully delivered, public education.

He says, "Excuse me, I don't mean to be rude
But I do not know what to call you.
Is it physically challenged, mobility impaired?
wheelchair bound, wheelchair user?
Handicapped, handicapper, handicappable?
crip, crippled, confined?
deformed, defective, disabled?
Inconvenienced, invalid?
sick, special, survivor?
Please tell me, what's the word?
What. . . ."
I say, "Wait! How about calling me by my name?"

His name is Johnson Cheu. Twenty-two and a half years ago, Johnson arrived, premature. He was placed inside an incubator for eighty days and, at some awful moment, a technical malfunction deprived Johnson's brain cells of oxygen.

"I've just been very fortunate," he tells me. "I have a very light case of spastic cerebral palsy. That means that a lot of my muscles never relax from varying states of permanent contraction."

I have never seen Johnson out of a wheelchair and I ask if spastic cerebral palsy dictates the use of such support. "Not exactly," he says. "I can, actually, stand and walk around. But I'm limited by the fact that one of my steps is the energy-expended equivalent of two hundred and sixty-five steps of yours. The chair increases my endurance, my mobility."

In his last semester as an undergraduate, Johnson served as a voluntary tutor for Berkeley High School students. Today he teaches four different English classes there and, once or twice a day, he breaks for a cup of coffee or a bottle of juice from the cafeteria where Charlie Lubin is gainfully employed.

Besides teaching, Johnson writes poetry and leads a University of California–Berkeley poetry workshop. He will enter Stanford University next September and pursue an accelerated graduate-studies program to receive secondary teaching credentials and a Master's in the Art of Education.

Charlie Lubin and Johnson Cheu are two of the forty-three million Americans who persist among us despite the burdens of mental or physical disability.

Day after day, Charlie and Johnson meet with ignorant/fearful/indifferent and cruel stupidities of response that most of us commit whenever we notice somebody markedly different from ourselves. Terms such as "retarded" or "crippled" plainly express our panic or our disdain.

Johnson Cheu has written a poem about the daily indignities he faces, describing the "hateful grimace" or the "sad pity eyes" that meet him when he goes shopping. He refuses to ask for assistance because he knows people will respond "in baby talk/pat my head." "I am not a dog," he writes.

On campus one afternoon, I stood chatting with Johnson Cheu. Suddenly a huge moving van began to back into us. We yelled as loud as we could, but the van wheezed and rolled closer and closer. Johnson had to execute some almost magical, swift maneuvering of his wheelchair in order to escape. We were both breathless and furious when, finally, we could stop scrambling for safety.

People don't give a damn. People do not think about the stamina demanded of anyone disabled. We hardly ever bother to imagine what it takes to get dressed, or to cook, or to eat, or to learn algebra, or to cross the street, if you are not 100 percent able-bodied. Disability means difficult and tedious and isolated and outcast.

BUT CHARLIE LUBIN and Johnson Cheu have won for themselves a way out of no way. In 1991, the Americans with Disabilities Act (ADA) became law. ADA easily compares to the most important civil-rights legislation of the 1960s. Most situations of employment and public facilities (from schoolrooms to hotels to airport telephones) must no longer discriminate against disabled persons. Legal concepts of discrimination now include physical design and redesign requirements as well as new consumer and/or employee and/or citizen-at-large policies. The intent of the law is to fully enable the disabled to function on a competitive, decently self-sufficient basis. This is the best anything to emerge from the U.S. Congress since I don't know when.

And so I hope we get on with the next task of enforcement, and make that happen fast. I hope we properly perceive this legislative precedent as solid ground for the shock of further good news: further revolutionary legislation that, for example, will enable the homeless and the sick to acquire the help they need, without humiliation.

If we will pay attention to the achievements of Charlie Lubin and Johnson Cheu, and if we will embrace and build upon the ADA, then, maybe, we will become part of some national good news that will lessen our national reasons for shame.

I Am Seeking

an Attitude

⋺⋵

1993

UNTIL NOW, I have never said, "I am a woman." I'm not sure why. I guess I'm not sure exactly what those words mean.

And yet my gender identity is as basic, as incontrovertible, as my racial identity. I have written the sentence "I am Black" innumerable times. I have thought that sentence, and I have felt its meaning all the way to the bone of my self.

What is the difference between gender and race? Why do I feel perfectly comfortable saying, "I am a Black woman," or "I am a woman of color," but then something inside me pretty serious balks/blanks out when it comes to the more elementary declaration: "I am a woman"?

Or why do I write without hesitation about the injustice that freed the cops who beat up Rodney King, and then I keep to myself my qualms about the fact that he has been charged with beating up his wife?

Maybe it has to do with the human necessity of pride.

We women are the majority of every people on the planet. But, everywhere, we are most lacking in political representation, least compensated for the work we do, most illiterate, most impoverished, most lacking in legal protection and recourse, and most concentrated in the lowest paying, least secure, and least valued sectors of the labor force.

In addition, we are, everywhere, subject to physical and social violence. On our own: On the streets of the world and in the dwelling places we call home, we are not safe. And, even in the realm of medicine and medical research, we, women, in general, do not exist: Most tests are conducted on men for diseases affecting primarily men. Men are regarded as the universal body, the universal voice. From cholesterol to literature, you just have to hope that your female organs and/or your female perspectives do not differ importantly from those organs and viewpoints of the universal male.

While this state of affairs can have readily comical results, it can also kill you—if you happen to be somebody who needs to say, "I am a woman."

For example, given the popular perception and sentiment on the horrifying crisis of AIDS, you would probably run into real trouble trying to educate people to the fact that breast cancer kills far, far more Americans every year. Over the past ten years, roughly 140,000 Americans have died of AIDS while close to 600,000 Americans have died of breast cancer. And yet, when President Bill Clinton got around to something specific about health care, in his budget speech to the nation, he rightly declared himself determined to greatly increase funding for AIDS research, but he did not so much as mention breast cancer.

Of course, breast cancer kills only women.

I am a woman. I am looking for reasons for pride in my gender identity. Given the international and the whole human historical context of female inequality, where can I find them?

Why did it take my mother so long to defend herself against my father? Why was suicide her final defense?

Why have we taken so long to defend ourselves against the

brutality, derision, and economic subjugation that have been our regular female experience?

Where are the reasons for pride?

Where are the woman songs comparable to ". . . and before I'll be a slave I'll be buried in my grave"?

And what about those of us asked to become—or bullied into becoming—the slave of the slave? What about we, women of color, who have been pained into a false choice between unconditional loyalty to our men (themselves despised by white men) and our own need to escape from despicable "bitch" status and treatment?

And why do men hate us, anyway? And why do we, nevertheless, and always, continue to love them as lovers and husbands, and fathers, and why do we women, as mothers, raise boys into a manhood that then endangers our own lives?

I AM SEEKING an attitude. Twenty years ago, I thought I was proving something terrific and really big deal when I decided I would, without exception, move through the corridors of Yale University in high heels and in as fashionable an array of dresses as I could almost afford on my unequal, woman's salary as an assistant professor. That was a weird episode of considerable discomfort. And it is curious to me, today, to realize that I thought I needed high heels and dresses to confirm my gender identity inside that ossified space of male values—and that I thought that such gender confirmation of myself, as a woman, would naturally mean something positive and good.

Boy, was I young!

Twenty years later, and I look through my file folders: Africa, Clinton, the Budget, African-American Issues, South Central L.A., Gay and Lesbian Issues, Foreign Policy Issues, and, yes, here is one labeled, WOMEN.

As I riffle through newspaper clippings kept under that heading, I can feel a kind of pitiless nausea overtaking me. Here is the African woman of Somalia who weighs forty-five pounds. Here are Muslim women clutching at such protection as they can find inside traditional Islam. Here are young Black teenagers (female), 62 percent of them likely to live below the poverty line once they drop out of high school—compared to 37 percent of young Black teenagers (male).

And, in any event, according to the *New York Times,* "Students sit in classrooms that, day in, day out, deliver the message that women's lives count for less than men's." Here are American women 50 percent more likely to be raped inside the military than in civilian life.

And here are more than 20,000 mostly Muslim women systematically suffering gang rape around the clock in the former Yugoslavia. And here is nobody powerful in this country, from President Clinton up or down, opening his—or her—mouth to decry these atrocities and to make them stop happening.

I mean, I am a woman.

And I am living and I am paying serious taxes inside this country that took us into an unholy, barbarous, unpardonable war against the people of Iraq for the sake of an inarguably plain old rotten dictatorship called Kuwait. And this country where I live and pay serious taxes murdered way more than hundreds of thousands of Iraqi human beings and spent way more than the total allocation for education on the delivery of such a savage rescue of such a stupid and intractable dictatorship as the one that still holds power in Kuwait. And yet—and yet!—the elected leadership of this same country where I live and where I pay serious taxes cannot even open its mouth to condemn genocidal rape!

This country cannot suddenly shoot its Patriot missiles and fly its Stealth bombers the hell into Serbian turf because . . . why? There is no oil in former Yugoslavia. And another thing: The only people being raped are women.

I am a woman. And I am seeking an attitude. I am trying to find reasons for pride.

I was proud when we elected four new women to the United States Senate.

I was proud when we elected the first Black woman to the United States Senate.

I was proud when a woman became Secretary of Health and Human Services.

I was proud when a woman became Attorney General of the United States.

But where are they now? Is it possible that not one of these illustrious women could find two minutes in which she could lay down humanitarian and, yes, military demands in behalf of the 20,000-plus mostly Muslim girls and women in former Yugoslavia?

Maybe they don't remember rape. Maybe when you get to be powerful you lose your gender identity above the neck and you just can't remember the very common horror of rape.

I am a woman. I have been raped twice in my life. And I remember. And I go through the hours of a Monday or a Tuesday and I do not forget what is happening to all the victims of so-called ethnic cleansing and, particularly, I do not forget the women victims of so-called ethnic cleansing. And I do not and I will not forgive the elected leadership of my country for its inertia and its silence and, therefore, its complicity with the evil of so-called ethnic cleansing.

WHERE ARE MY reasons for pride? One of my colleagues, in a manner of speaking, Anna Quindlen, recently published a column arguing for intervention in behalf of these female victims of rape. Ordinarily, I respect and admire Anna Quindlen's writing. But for her, rape was not the point. Rather the tragedy is this: Having been raped and raped and raped and raped, again and again, these thousands upon thousands of young mostly Muslim girls and women may never become receptive to any future proposition of heterosexual intercourse and, hence, these rape victims may be unable and/or unwilling to serve a procreative function for their people.

And, hence, these people, 100 percent, may perish.

I guess I should say, "Thank God Quindlen managed some justification for the rescue of these female casualties of so-called ethnic cleansing."

But is it not remarkable, is it not appalling, that she, evidently, does not believe that rape, by itself, is quite sufficiently something to interdict because rape, by itself, is horribly destructive, violent, and wrong?

Where are her reasons for pride?

Or mine—when, in the past, I have argued for our equality and empowerment mainly by emphasizing our indispensable procreative and then our nurturing functions?

How low can we go?

Pretty damned low-down when I must present the issues of my freedom and my rights primarily in the context of my ongoing usefulness to somebody else!

I am a woman. And that's not easy.

Crazies out here want to tell me all about my body. My body! Tell me no abortion. Try to kill any doctor who could help me. Went and killed one. Finally. Blew him away. Three bullets shredding the flesh of his back. Crazies out here blowing up/closing down abortion clinics. Call me Welfare Queen if I go ahead and have the babies when I don't have no job and no way to get a job and nowhere to leave the babies if I do find something anyhow.

Crazies out here tell me I can't love no woman. Want to kill me if I do. Went and killed one. Hattie Cohens in Salem, Oregon. Burned her to death.

Crazies out here tell me I can't love no man unless he have himself a big-time income and reliably conjugal inclinations. Crazies out here tell me I can't love no man unless we married anyway. The Pope say just abstain. The Pope himself abstain.

Crazies out here like to drive me crazy.

But I'm not crazy. I am seeking an attitude.

Out of these histories of horror and impositions of shame and degradations of a rising freedom spirit, is there a pathway to my pride? Behind that question is another one. Is there a will to power?

For me, the problem of gender identity stems from its usual estrangement from ambitions of power. Usually we push for things to change in our favor, yes, but usually we push in the most courteous and reasonable and listening fashion imaginable. We want or we need whatever it is because that would be the right thing, the moral case, and because, otherwise, we are left in danger and in pain.

Hardly ever do we enter the realms of righteous rage! Hardly ever do we formulate the matter so that whoever opposes or impedes or ridicules our demands will understand that if he does not get out of our way and or get rid of that smirk he will be the one in danger: He will be the one in pain!

Hardly ever do we make it clear that by "rights" we mean power: The power of deterrence and the power of retaliation and the power to transform our societies so that no longer and never again shall more than half of every people on the planet beg for dignity and safe passage and political and economic equality!

Usually we try to persuade or seduce or defuse the anxieties or deflect the violence of our opposition. Usually we try to fool ourselves, as well: The War Against Women surely does not require War Against the Enemies of Women—be they male or female. And so we neither win nor lose; we persist—and too often we perish. At the very least, we perish in the spirit.

For me, the problem of gender identity is our evasion of the implications of power and our may-I-say-"feminine" inclinations to make nice. War is not nice. And it's hard to embrace something alive and yet powerless. It's even a bit creepy as an idea: something alive without power. But female gender identity, per se, has been presented like that, to me. It has been given to me as a certificate of suffering: I am one of those who could have been thrown away or suffocated or drowned at birth because I was born a girl.

But pride does not arise from suffering. Pride develops as we resist our misery, as we revolt against, and as we exorcise all misery from our days and nights.

And so I know pride as a Black woman and as a woman of color because Black people and people of color resist oppression and because we loathe, actively, every source of our unequal liberty, our unequal entitlement under law.

We behold our racial identity as a call to arms, a summoning of ourselves into battle for power and territory and wealth and happiness and well-being. We declare war against our enemies. We wage war for the sake of our self-determination.

"We," in this case of colored peoples, includes me.

But have we, women of these United States, for example, have we declared war against our enemies? Are we ready to live and die for the sake of our self-determination?

• • •

SHOW ME THE nationwide day of absence by women so that, for starters, the Equal Rights Amendment shall become law.

Show me female vigilante patrols keeping city streets and country roads safe for our passage at any time and in any attire of our choosing.

Show me national flying furies who confront and who overpower crazy Operation Rescue gangsters wherever they dare to raise their ugly killer heads.

Show me proportional political representation of women by women on every level of government.

Show me women loving women absolutely without persecution and absolutely without death.

Show me overdue changes so that everyone who does such "women's work" as day care of children and night care of children and teaching and nursing and peace-making and converting the wilderness of our humanly mixed attributes into a benign environment for human beings—everyone who does this so-called women's work shall receive more money and more perks than General Colin Powell or your nearest college football coach.

Show me emergency federal commitment to cure breast cancer.

Show me our feminist faxorama to jam White House machinery with our demands for crisis intervention against rape in former Yugoslavia and against violence against women in our own country.

Show me the power and I will feel the pride!

I am a woman. And I think I have found my attitude. And I think, really, it's about: "Let's get it on!"

THE TRUTH OF
RODNEY KING

><

1993

APRIL 17, 1993, and a federal jury has found two Los Angeles policemen guilty in the beating of Rodney King twenty-five months ago. This same jury found the other two police defendants not guilty. And, immediately, attorneys for the convicted have declared their intention to appeal. So, today, there is less than a full-fledged national disgrace recurring in Los Angeles.

But we would be ill advised to assume that even this partial delivery of justice will stand. And we would be oblivious to brutal colonial attitudes if we did not note and decry that the overwhelming state response to the first miscarriage of justice has been paramilitary, at best. There has been no top priority of focus and thinktank frenzy to relieve the beleaguered citizens of South Central Los Angeles with money and programs that could lift them out of the violence of poverty and the violence of unequal protection under the law.

Nothing basic has changed. And so my spirit remains riveted, still, with grief and misgivings, to one year ago: On April 29, 1992, the whole world learned of the Simi Valley verdict of "not guilty" in the first trial of the Los Angeles policemen accused of brutally beating an unarmed African-American man named Rodney King.

My own initial reaction to this terrible and completely shocking news was to burst into tears of bitterness and terror: In my lifetime, will violence ever be made to stop inside the national Black community? In my lifetime, will the American system of justice ever deliver anything besides injustice to the Black community?

Because there had been a videotape documentary of the police assault on Rodney King, I had expected, along with millions of other African-Americans, that for once the guilty would be punished and the victim would be protected by due process under the law. But the visual documentary evidence of unlawful police violence—evidence that was sickening to watch even at the remove of a TV set—that evidence did not carry the day. Racism carried the day.

According to a defense attorney, hideous, monster images of Black men as wild and depraved subhuman creatures motivated Los Angeles police to attack one unarmed African-American man with nauseating and relentless savagery.

And where did the police acquire such racist images?

Is it not the case that American media coverage of young Black men promotes such violent, such vicious fantasy?

Is it not the case that, as Malcolm X observed, media coverage of Blackfolks serves to criminalize the Black community in the minds of white America and, having criminalized our community, police violence against our communities appears justified and necessary to most Americans?

Is it not the case that the lamentable nature of our usual school curriculum is such that most white Americans, most Asian-Americans, most Latino-Americans, and even a sadly significant number of African-Americans, ourselves, do not learn anything important and accurate about African-American history, or culture, and so in the absence of coherent, valid, historical instruction, all of these various Americans accept the cultural perversities of media coverage as objective, reliable, and truthful information?

It was that very same one unarmed African-American man, Rodney King, the victim of inarguable and unlawful police savagery, it was he who said through the microphones of the press that rushed to cover the L.A. uprising against the injustice of the Simi Valley verdict, "Please can we get along here. . . . We all can get along. I mean, we're all stuck here for a while. Let's try to work it out."

These were the words of the Black man who, allegedly, so terrified the L.A. police that they could not help but beat and stomp him almost to death. You would think that, perhaps, the truth of his being that spoke to his countrymen beginning with the word "please" might well explode and exorcise the racist fantasies and misinformation and ignorance that underlay the police assault upon his defenseless body.

But that would be a woeful underestimation of the racist nature of Rodney King's predicament. That would be a willful blindness to the racist nature of the national response to the L.A. uprising against the depravity of judgment that led to the "not guilty" verdict in the first trial.

The truth of Rodney King and the truth of African America is not anything that racist America intends to allow, or learn, or teach, or protect.

The truth of Rodney King and the truth of African America is an integral part of the truth of the emerging new majority of these United States: a majority that is neither white nor necessarily English speaking. In less than sixty years, most Americans will be descendants of the peoples of Africa, Asia, the Pacific Islands, the Hispanic world, and Arabia, not Europe.

Where is the public school curriculum that is ready to teach all of these new Americans what they need and deserve to know about themselves, and about each other?

How can anybody justify compulsory public schooling and yet deny the racial and ethnic reality of the students compelled to sit inside our classrooms?

Despite media coverage of the L.A. uprising, it is a fact that most of the people arrested were Hispanic, not Black. Forty percent of businesses destroyed were Hispanic, and most of the rest of the businesses destroyed were owned by Korean-Americans.

Where is the public school curriculum that is ready to teach these three communities—African-Americans, Asian-Americans, and Latino-Americans—how our histories intersect and how our bound-together destinies depend upon our ignorance or our knowledge of our connections: our common oppressor, as Malcolm X would put it?

If we could gather together the political force of African- and Asian- and Latino-American communities, if we could coalesce these peoples into one lobby for educational reform, a national housing program, and job training for jobs that exist, we could empower the numerical new majority of Americans and become the political new majority.

Since 1970, twenty million Asians and Latinos have emigrated to America. But, so far, the necessary American redefinition of race and the necessary American revolution of public education in America—a redefinition and a revolution required by this enormous infusion of new, non-European human life into our mainstream—so far these transformations have not happened. And so far these communities have competed and contended for a pitiful slice of leftover pie. Coalitions have yet to come together.

A N D   S O I would like to respond to Rodney King. I would like to say, yes, we can all get along—but first we will have to coalesce in order to enlarge that pitiful slice into a whole, big, massive pie. And second, we will have to coalesce in order to secure the revolution of America's public schools so that the faces and the names and the languages of our children demand that we change the meaning of "we" and that justice and equality in the courtroom, in the streets, on the job, and in the classroom are, as Martin Luther King, Jr., would say, the best guarantors—the only guarantors—of our "getting along."

First, let me deal with the pie:

In Ron Takaki's brilliant book, *A Different Mirror,* he cites these lines written by a Japanese immigrant describing a lesson learned by Mexican and Asian farm laborers in California: "People harvesting work together unaware of racial problems." But as we know only too well, since 1970 there has been less and less to harvest here in America.

Since 1970, we have had to survive a calculated federal withering of every program capable of ending poverty, or mitigating the misery of poverty. Since 1970, we have been forced to survive huge federal cuts in aid to our cities, cuts in public education, cuts in the care of the sick, cuts in drug rehabilitation. And we have had to survive the massive deterioration of our bridges and our roadways and our public facilities even as we have had to survive the massive deterioration of the best hopes of our young people and the massive deterioration of our economy as a means of support and purpose and security for our American lives.

Those twenty million new Americans who arrived from 1970 onward came here from Mexico and from El Salvador and from Vietnam and from Korea and from Japan because, just like the seventeenth-century pilgrims, they were desperate for a better life. But they arrived just as an official white backlash against African-Americans was going into high, inhuman gear.

And so these past two decades have seen an enormous swelling of citizen need coincident with an entirely cruel, shortsighted, unjust, and always racist construction of citizen opportunities and citizen entitlement.

This is why there is just a pitiful slice of leftover pie.

Second, we will have to coalesce in order to secure the revolution of America's public schools. We must demand recognition of the faces and the names and the languages of our culture. Those of us who have been designated for so long as special interest/fringe group/minorities—we have the happiness now of realizing that we have become the mainstream; we are the people.

We: African-Americans and Latino-Americans and Asian-Americans and Native Americans and Pacific Islanders and Arab-Americans and women and gay Americans and lesbian Americans and Americans with disabilities—that is the new American meaning of "we," that is the de facto coalition that put Bill Clinton into the White House. We constitute a de facto coalition responsible for electing the current President of these United States.

We are truly powerful! And now we must move from de facto coalition to self-conscious, aggressively activist coalition and take over the classrooms and take over the American core curriculum of public education.

THIS MEANS, for one thing, that we must laugh or fight the so-called controversy over so-called politically correct instruction out of our lives.

And if we could provide these new Asian- and Latino-Americans with the accurate and coherent historical information that they need—if we could properly educate these new Americans, then they would know, for example, that their own heartbreaking predicament of rejection and hate crime and taxation without representation and poverty and startlingly high rates of tuberculosis and suicide—their newfound American predicament—directly derives from the ongoing, hateful predicament of African-Americans against whom racist white America raised a federal backlash meant to whip Blackfolks into invisibility and silent suffering.

And if we could provide African-Americans with the accurate and coherent historical information that they need, then African-Americans would understand the completely legitimate, kindred aspirations of these new immigrants, understand the persecuted histories their emigration bespeaks, and understand our heavy, real connections to these new Americans.

But can we provide such an education?

I say we must. And I say we can, absolutely.

We must organize the parents of our students. We must teach the parents of our students so that they will join hands with us to defeat every single so-called "school voucher" proposal that comes up—wherever it comes up!

We must organize and teach the parents of our students what that school voucher brainstorm is all about. We must make it unmistakably clear that the idea behind that brainstorm is this: Since the

American public is changing so that the so-called minorities now constitute the majority population in our public schools, it is time to eviscerate public education in order to protect the new white *minority* of Americans: Take away the money, and we will have to close the schools and/or close the libraries and/or use completely obsolete and indefensible textbooks and/or crowd the classrooms so that teachers must resign for the sake of their sanity.

When public education served the powerful, it was compulsory, and money flowed into the coffers of our schools. Now that public education must challenge and displace the currently powerful—or else betray its obligations to its new American clients—the currently powerful oppose and seek to weaken and to destroy the validity of public schools on which the overwhelming majority of young Americans must rely for their empowerment.

Today we have California Governor Pete Wilson saying ridiculous things like, we must increase community college tuition by 300 percent. Today we see teachers in Los Angeles bullied into a so-called vote about whether to take a 10 percent cut or lose their jobs altogether. That, I submit, is not a vote, *not* a choice. That is a shameful episode in our state and in our country.

We must reject outright any and all pay cuts for teachers. Let's get serious about who is doing the work. Let the members of Congress and the governors and the chancellors and the football coaches—let them take a 50 percent pay cut!

It is lunatic to ask of teachers any further sacrifice. It is lunatic to tolerate any further erosion of the well-being and capability of our public education system in America.

Just as President Clinton recently pledged $17 billion in new money to the high-tech industry, he needs to commit an additional $20 billion to the industry of public education.

YES, BUT WHERE is the money to come from? President Clinton has said that there are no sacred cows in his budget. But I beg to differ:

The 1992 Defense Department received $307 billion of our

money. That's 20 percent of the total budget. And the $307 billion stipulated does not even include veterans' benefits.

And what about education?

The 1992 U.S. budget allocated $45 billion to education—and job training, too, that is.

I say there is a sacred cow in the picture.

A B-2 bomber costs $2 billion—each. Let's have a B-2 bomber for the public school system of every single city in America: $20 billion in additional money for education would mean only ten fewer B-2 bombers on the runway to nowhere.

President Clinton has said it is time to invest in America. I agree, completely. Which is the better investment: ten B-2 bombers, or $20 billion in additional money, *our money,* for the physical refurbishment and democratic reform and academic revolution of American education?

At this point we put 20 percent of our total budget into bomber planes and missiles while Germany and Japan put 5 percent of their respective budgets into "defense." Where is the mystery of our inability to compete?

The Cold War is over, the Berlin Wall is down. What the hell are we defending against?

We need to call our own Senators and Representatives. We need to call Bill and Hillary Clinton and tell them to cook that sacred cow. We are starving out here!

Now, supposing we get a B-2 bomber for every public school system of every city in America. That's $2 billion a pop.

Then supposing we use that money to duly remunerate American teachers of American children so that, at last, our teachers receive the financial and social respect they deserve—as the literal, designated mentors for our national destiny.

And supposing that we succeed in transforming ourselves in our minds and in our deeds from minority and special or fringe-group members into an aggressive majority coalition of Americans determined to get real about this new America in our hands—and in our classrooms.

And supposing we successfully devise a core curriculum that includes the whole world and all of America rather than something else—something quite familiar and dangerous and useless and wrong.

And supposing then that we learn what we need to learn in order to teach our students about themselves—that is to say, teach them about American diversity, which is the beginning and the test-ending truth of these United States.

Then, can we all get along?

In Martin Luther King's essay, "A Testament of Hope," which was published after his assassination, he wrote:

"When millions of people have been cheated for centuries, restitution is a costly process. Inferior education, poor housing, unemployment, inadequate health care—each is a bitter component of the oppression that has been our heritage. Each will require billions of dollars to correct. Justice so long deferred has accumulated interest and its cost for this society will be substantial in financial as well as human terms. This fact has not been grasped, because most of the gains of the past decade were obtained at bargain prices. The desegregation of public housing cost nothing; neither did the election and appointment of a few black public officials. . . .

"The black revolution is much more than a struggle for the rights of Negroes. It is forcing America to face all its interrelated flaws—racism, poverty, militarism, and materialism. . . . It reveals systemic rather than superficial flaws and suggests that radical reconstruction of society itself is the real issue to be forced."

I PROPOSE THAT we begin by facing the political nature of education, the political nature of knowledge, and our collective power to change what our children know about themselves and about each other so that we can get along with the business of saving the world for human life.

I propose that we underscore to ourselves and to our elected representatives and to our students and to our civilian police force that the achievement of a great society depends upon securing justice and equality for all of its citizens.

I propose that we redesign our political and our academic and our social lives so that we can finally answer that one unarmed African-American man, Rodney King, saying to him, well, yes, we can all get along as soon as we take care of some serious business—on your behalf and mine, and ours.

We have to join with every American who would love justice and equality more than a law-and-order status quo of hidden but combustible inequities and chasmic, silent suffering.

And, then, yes, we can all get along.

Yes, please God: I believe we can.

Islam and the USA Today

1993

THE WOMAN WEIGHS forty-six pounds. She is too thin to breathe. What's left of her flesh barely covers her bones. Her eyes persist as soft as they are large and brown. She is African. She is probably Muslim. She is dying in Somalia, the country of her birth. In the last six months, hundreds of thousands of Somalis have already died. Children have perished in huge numbers difficult to admit.

Or, those who were captured were twelve to twenty-five years old. Some of them managed to escape from vile detention camps where more than ten thousand girls and young women remain, repeatedly raped by day and by night. Many of them are Muslim. They are casualties of an "ethnic cleansing" that imperils all of the Muslims alive in former Yugoslavia.

Or, on barren land between Lebanon and Israel, four hundred men arrived in winter and emptiness. They had been blindfolded and pushed into buses that traveled through the darkness, with illegal speed. They had been seized inside their homes and driven away, at gunpoint, into sudden unimaginable exile. From their enemies each of them received a blanket, a paper bag of food, and fifty dollars. They are Palestinians. Most are Muslims. They may not survive. No man can live on no man's land.

Or, roughly two years ago, we launched one of the most relentless and savage bombing assaults in human history. Our target was the city of Baghdad, home to 6.5 million people, mostly Muslim. Even now, that voiceless and beleaguered population must contend with the ferocious consequences of our attack: widespread disease, severe malnutrition, contaminated water, and nationwide cultural and technological wipeout.

Or, during the holiday transition from 1992 to 1993, one of the mainstays of local entertainment was Walt Disney's animated feature film, *Aladdin*. Except for the hero and the villain, all the men are corpulent and ugly. All the women, including the heroine, appear, throughout, half naked and/or clad in nearly transparent "harem" attire à la Hollywood. The villain turned out to be "a dark man" thinking "dark thoughts." Given the ostensible story line, one assumes that every character is an Arab and, therefore, Muslim. I cannot imagine Black people, or Jews, or anybody other than Arab men and women, drawn in such repulsive, frightening, vapid, and inaccurate fashion, today, without enormous popular and political uproar.

Or, the media gave far more coverage to the "amicable" break between Charles and Diana than they devoted to the terrifying and internecine explosion of violence and counterviolence between the Hindu majority and the Muslim minority of India. Nowhere could you find any depth of analysis or appropriate background information. For example, how many Americans understand Britain's colonial responsibility, as regards this latest bloody and tragic outbreak of intraracial hostilities? How many of us know that more Muslims live in India than in Pakistan?

And what does that matter?

WHILE HE WAS spokesman for the Black Nation of Islam, Malcolm X aroused the self-respect of Blackfolks otherwise impervious to organized appeals for unity and discipline. After his pilgrimage to Mecca, Malcolm became an orthodox Muslim and, among other things, his experience of Islam deracialized his basic take on moral reality.

Who is Muslim and what is Islam?

Or, where does Islam fit "inside" American objectives for the twenty-first century?

As religion rises into the incendiary realm of world affairs, we should take care to detect and oppose, de facto and aforethought, U.S. wars against the people of Islam. In the instance of Somalia and former Yugoslavia, we can verify the impact of our aggression through inertia. In the instances of Iraq and the Palestinians, White House perspectives have led to overt assault, decimation, and unacknowledged, awful suffering.

The first so-called Christian crusade was anything but holy, anything but benign. In the name of their exclusive beliefs, Western white men, again and again, invaded distant Muslim towns and cities. These first "crusaders" slaughtered all of the "infidels" they encountered in these "infidel" homelands. What is happening now?

The hour is already dreadful, and late, for self-examination of the unfolding, unholy nature of regular American response to Muslim men and women in various extremities of need or self-definition and affirmation. Islam will not fit itself into White House daydreams of "a new world order." Accordingly, we had better get ready to decide, on an altogether public and conscious level, what we, what the USA, plans to do, or not do, about that.

At the moment, we pretend to ignorance of our crimes and we proceed on the basis of racist ignorance of the victims of our crimes.

And the Muslim woman of Somalia weighs forty-six pounds. What is her name? Why is she starving to death? And what names will she call you and me if she ever regains her strength to speak out loud?

And how shall we defend to ourselves our behavior in the context of her needs/her human rights? What is the moral meaning of our own gods?

BOSNIA BETRAYED

⊰⊱

1993

I USED TO WONDER what it must have felt like to be a grown-up living in Germany or in the United States during World War II. How did anybody hear about the Nazis? Did everyone believe the news? Did anybody care?

I always wanted to imagine that only bad people didn't know what was happening; only bad people could choose to ignore or else accommodate to evil. This had to mean that regular good people locked arms within minutes of the first reports and then powerful good people went without food and sleep until they figured out what to do. And then, of course, they did it: They moved whatever and whomever needed to be moved to stop the genocide.

But today was cloudy. And tonight it's raining. At dinner, I had to accept or reject a small piece of lemon pie, and then I had to decide for or against a second slice. Mostly, this is the way I live:

watching the weather, and making decisions of extremely little consequence.

My friends are not much different. One of them just flew back from a boring job interview in Colorado, and to celebrate his return, we played tennis for an hour. Another friend turned fifty, and well-wishers came around for birthday barbecue.

But every night, I keep waking up. There is now a visible rash on my neck. Is this the trivial big picture in which yet another Muslim girl is savagely attacked and raped? Is this the pedestrian frame of reference in which yet another Muslim village explodes in flames? More than twenty thousand Muslim girls and young women repeatedly and repeatedly raped!

Systematic rape makes me nauseated, even as an idea. And I am dark. I'm Black, in fact. And a whole lot of folks find me and mine definitely undesirable. And I do not require some megadose of anything to imagine me and mine the object of "ethnic cleansing," and I really have a problem with a program like that. I really do.

And I cannot understand why people wonder about what kind of health care Bill Clinton will finally propose, or if he will ever forget about the deficit and focus, for example, on South Central L.A. If "ethnic cleansing" doesn't get to you, if the comic-book specter of Ross Perot is more disturbing to you than the documented and relentlessly ruinous assault of Muslim girls and young women, then things are pretty clear. There is nothing to wonder about.

BILL CLINTON, who cravenly capitulates his constitutional civilian power to the military, utterly lacks a value system hinged to the survival of human life and dignity, which is why he buddies up with Colin Powell.

And Powell! Did he luck out or what? When Clinton was elected, he probably thought he had become the dutiful employee of a President with whom he might regularly disagree. But no! Now he finds himself the Big Boy in the picture: the man to be mollified and coddled and photographed with.

Powell was a poor student at City College years ago, and today, in the context of gay and lesbian rights, he clearly does not remember Harry Truman ordering the military to integrate. That made possible Powell's very own j-o-b. But his job is the least of it.

Evidently, Powell does not remember the Middle Passage that carried millions of Africans captured for slavery to these shores. He does not remember how many more millions of his African forefathers and foremothers perished during that bedeviled voyage. He does not recall how, once the surviving victims reached America, a national policy of "ethnic cleansing" beginning with slave codes beleaguered our days and our nights from that awful moment of arrival to this moment. Does he?

Isn't he the humanitarian genius who concocted the plan to deliver food to Bosnian Muslims by dropping ten-ton packages from jet planes thousands of feet up in the sky?

Isn't he the tough guy whose idea of a good fight is Grenada or another round of infernal bombing of Baghdad, in famished, disease-ridden Iraq?

Isn't he the courageous military counselor advising Clinton to stay out of former Yugoslavia because maybe there might be an American fighter plane shot down or American troops wounded, and so forth?

Thank God Powell and Clinton did not head the country during World War II. We were unconscionably slow getting into it but, at last, and at least, we did get into it.

To coexist with genocide is to collaborate with genocide. "Ethnic cleansing" implies and glorifies genocide. More than 120,000 Bosnian Muslim men, women, and children slaughtered! More than a million and a half Muslims terrorized into refugee flight!

What will compel national and international commitment of every kind of resource available to stop the brutality and the genocide?

If we do not rescue Bosnian Muslims from their rapine executioners, if we do not restore to them their rightful, sovereign territory, then how shall we justify our military might and our think-tank capacities?

Is there any cause more clear, more summoning, than the cause of human life?

Apparently, yes. And, therefore, there is no safety for any of us: no safety. Nor do we deserve to suppose that we should be safe when the intended extermination of another people does not disturb our routine preoccupations.

Yes, but if we went into Bosnia, what about other situations of similar horror? Wouldn't we have to intervene all over the place? . . .

You bet. And so what about that! I mean, excuse me, but are we or are we not talking about "ethnic cleansing"? Are we or are we not talking about somebody violently seizing space that belongs to some-one else—*someone not clean enough to live?*

Exactly who is clean enough to stay alive? Exactly who should decide who's clean and who's dirty/wrong/off/dark/undesirable?

H E Y, I W O U L D like to return to my quandary about slices of lemon pie. And I would like to devote myself to loving somebody who loves me. And there is music I need to hear. And flowers I need to see. And children I want to hold close to my heart. And these homely desires define a delicate human condition that cannot with-stand our indifference, our inertia, our insensibility when somebody else is screaming for help in his and her house.

At the least and at this horribly late date I say it's time to retrieve our national moneys from our armed forces: Armed forces not at the disposal of human life are indefensible.

Let us aggressively retrieve those ill-spent moneys and spend them in ways that may begin to enable us to be and act like human beings down and dirty for the rightful, dignified survival of us all.

FREEDOM TIME

>=<

1993

A MILLION YEARS AGO, Janis Joplin was singing, "Freedom's just another word for nothing left to lose." I found that puzzling, back then. Or, "white."

To my mind, freedom was an obvious good. It meant looking at an apartment and, if you liked it, being able to put down a deposit and sign a lease. It meant looking for a job and, if you found something for which you qualified—on the basis of education and/or experience—being able to take that position. Freedom had to do with getting into college if your grades were good enough. Freedom meant you could register to vote and live to talk about it.

A lot of other Americans felt the same way thirty years ago. And Black and white, we sang militant songs and we tested public transportation and restaurants and universities and corporate hiring policies and nice, clean neighborhoods for freedom. And we rallied and we marched and we risked everything for freedom because we believed that freedom would deliver us into pride and happiness and middle-class incomes and middle-class safety.

Thirty years later, and freedom is no longer a word that most folks remember to use, jokingly or otherwise. And the declining popularity of the word is matched by our declining commitment to protect, and to deepen, and to extend, the meanings of freedom in the United States.

Today we know that "Black and white" does not adequately describe anything real. Individual, economic, racial, ethnic, and sexual realities defy such long-ago simplicity. "Black" has become Nigerian or Afro-Caribbean or Senegalese or African-American or Zulu. "White" has become Serbo-Croatian or Bosnian Muslim or Irish Republican or Italian-American or Greek or Norwegian. And, even as collective identities inside America have multiplied, our political presence here has intensified as well: women, Latino, Asian, Native, gay, lesbian, senior citizen, and so-called legal and illegal aliens. (As for the very popular concept of "aliens," you would think that, by now, anybody other than Native Americans or Chicanos/Mexicans would be pretty embarrassed to mouth such an obnoxious pejorative.)

But rather than recognize galvanizing intersections among us, too often we yield to divisive media notions, such as women's rights, for example, threatening the rights of Blackfolks or Chicanos. There is a dismal competition among Americans who should know better and who should join together for their own good. There is an acquiescence in the worst knavery of the mass media, as those top TV shows and those major weekly magazines inflame our most egocentric and paranoid inclinations. In consequence, we are muddling through a terrifying period of atomization and bitterness and misdirected anger.

What the new emerging majority of these United States holds in common, at its core, is a need for freedom to exist equally and a need to become the most knowledgeable, happy, productive, interconnected, and healthy men and women that we can. Ours is a need for freedom that does not omit any racial, gender, ethnic, sexual, or physical identity from its protection. But unless we will, each of us, reach around all of these identities and embrace them even as we cherish our own, no one's freedom will be assumed.

In Margaret Atwood's novel *The Handmaid's Tale,* the reader comes upon this remarkable one-liner: "Nothing changes instantaneously: In a gradually heating bathtub, you'd be burned to death before you knew it." I think we're jammed inside that bathtub and the water's getting hot.

ABOUT FIVE WEEKS ago, I was walking my dog, Amigo, along the rather quiet streets of North Berkeley when a young white man yelled something in my direction and asked me to stop. I stopped. He bolted in front of me and, excitedly, inquired whether I had seen "anything or anyone unusual." I said no, and waited to hear him out.

It seems that twice on that one day, somebody had "delivered" an anti-Semitic bound book of neo-Nazi filth to the lawn in front of his house. He, Eric, was the father of a newborn baby and his Jewish wife, he told me, was completely freaked out by these scary events.

"How about you?" I asked him. Eric shrugged, and kept repeating that he "didn't understand it" and "couldn't believe" that none of his neighbors had seen anything. We talked a little while and I gave Eric my name and telephone number, as well as the numbers of some active people who might rally, fast, against this hatefulness.

In subsequent weeks, Eric invited me (and Amigo) into his house to meet his wife and to see their new baby boy, but I never had the time. Or, I never made the time to visit them.

SHORTLY AFTER the first delivery of neo-Nazi literature to my neighborhood, I got on a plane bound for Madison, Wisconsin. *The Progressive* was putting on a benefit show and the editors arranged for me to join the celebration. Madison, Wisconsin, is a lot like North Berkeley except Madison gets cold, and stays cold, during the winter. Similar to my Northern California habitat, there are abundant public indications of environmental concern and civility:

sheltered bus stops, wheel-chair-accessible street crossings, bike lanes, public tennis courts, fabulous public libraries, a wonderful public university, and bookstores and backpackers all over the place.

I stayed with Dr. Elizabeth Ann Karlin during my visit to Madison. The morning after my arrival, Dr. Karlin and I sat at the dining table looking at newspapers, drinking coffee, and pushing bagels away from the butter and the cream cheese. At some point, Dr. Karlin stopped talking, and I glanced at her face: It was flushed, and she fell silent. Now her dogs were wild with barking and ferocious agitation.

I got up and went to the windows. Outside, two white men were marching back and forth carrying placards that said, ABORTION: A BABY CAN LIVE WITHOUT IT, and LIBERTY AND JUSTICE FOR SOME.

Breakfast was over.

I located my press pass, my ballpoint pen, yellow pad, and I tied my sneaker shoelaces and went outside to interview these members of "Operation Rescue" and "Missionaries to the Pre-born." Why were they there?

"We're picketing Elizabeth Karlin's house because she kills babies in her Women's Medical Health Center."

I talked with Kermit Simpson and David Terpstra for more than two hours. It was eerie. It was familiar. They spoke about the futility of the courts, the brutality of the police, and their determination, regardless, to rescue "innocent babies" from "murder." It was familiar because their complaints and their moral certitude echoed the regular complaints and the moral certainty of the civil rights movement.

But these groups were white. These groups were right-wing religious fundamentalists. And the only freedom they were concerned about was the freedom of the "unborn."

In fact, throughout our lengthy conversation, neither one of these men ever referred to any woman or anything female: "The baby" had to be saved from murder. That was the formulation. No woman's mind or body or feelings or predicament, at any moment, entered their consideration. What mattered was "the baby."

As I listened to David Terpstra, a good-looking white man in his twenties, it occurred to me that he was the kind of person who might have shot and killed Dr. Gunn. Certainly he would see no reason not to kill a doctor who "kills babies." David told me there are twenty-two warrants out for his arrest, and he keeps moving.

He has no wife and no children and nothing special besides his mission to save "the baby."

Inside Dr. Karlin's house, the day was ruined. Even if the sun had returned to the sky (which it refused to do), there was terror and dread palpable, now, in every room.

And where were the good people of Madison who love their civil liberties and who hold Dr. Karlin in highest esteem as a warrior of our times and who used to understand that individual freedom depends upon a mass demand for its blessings and opportunities?

And what could I do for my friend, the doctor, before I got back on a plane, and left the scene of her clear and present danger?

THE NEXT WEEKEND was a memorial reading for Tede Matthews, a gay white American who had managed the Modern Times bookstore in San Francisco, and who had died of AIDS in July. Tede Matthews had also distinguished himself as an activist for human rights in Central America. And he had helped many, many writers and poets to acquire a community of support. He was/he is much beloved. And he died of AIDS.

In the overflow audience of several hundred people who came to honor Tede Matthews's life and to establish a Tede Matthews fund for civil rights for gay men and lesbians in Central America and in the United States, there were many gay men and lesbians.

And I heard in my brain the helter-skelter of selective scripture that the Operation Rescue guys hurled into that Wisconsin silence. And I reflected on the tragedy of Tede Matthews's death, and the death of thousands upon thousands of young men whom we have loved and lost. And I wanted to rise from my seat in a towering, prophetic rage and denounce any scripture/any construct of divinity that does not cherish all of the living people on earth and does not grieve for the cruelties of daily life that afflict every one of us if basic freedom is denied.

But this was a memorial service. And Tede Matthews is no longer alive.

ON MY RETURN to U.C.–Berkeley, one of my students alerted me to a forthcoming issue of *Mother Jones* that would trash Women's Studies in general and our department in particular. This student, Pamela Wilson, had been quoted out of context and she explained things to me. And she was mad.

The *Mother Jones* article proved to be a juicyfruit of irresponsible, sleazy journalism: a hatchet job with malice toward every facet of the subject under scrutiny and entitled, "Off Course."

Since its appearance, several other national publications have chimed in, applauding the "exposure" of "fraud" perpetrated upon students beguiled into taking courses that let them study themselves and sometimes sit in a circle of chairs.

The head of Women's Studies, Professor Evelyn Glenn, called a special departmental meeting. The faculty decided to respond to the attack, in writing, and on national public radio.

One student, Catherine Cook, has received hate mail from loquacious bigots who believe that women's studies, along with ethnic studies, make it clear that public education is wasting taxpayer money. Furthermore, these "nonacademic" studies "debase" the minds of young Americans who, instead, should "get a job," and so forth.

As a matter of fact, this latest assault on freedom of inquiry and the pivotal role of public education within that categorical mandate, this most recent effort to roll things back to "the basics" of white men studies taught by white men with the assistance of books written by and about white men has upset our students. The young woman who received hate mail because she thought she had a right to pursue her (women's) studies had trouble breathing, and her hands shook, as she brought those items of hatred into our faculty meeting. Students in my class, Coming Into the World Female, seemed puzzled, at first, and then stunned, and now furious with brilliant energies as they prepare for a press conference, a mock

Women's Studies class, and a demonstration that will take place just outside the entrance to the office building of *Mother Jones*.

The students voted to create those public reactions. They have spent hours and hours in solemn, wearisome research and composition. They believe that the truth of their intentions—and the truth of the necessity for women's studies and ethnic studies and African-American studies—will become apparent to most of America if only they, the students, do all of this homework into the facts, and if only they give the design and the wording of their flyers maximal painstaking and meticulous execution.

They believe that there is a mainstream majority America that will try to be fair, and that will respect their courage, and admire the intelligence of their defense. They believe that there is a mainstream majority America that will overwhelm the enemies of public and democratic education. They believe that most of us, out here, will despise and resist every assault on freedom in the United States.

And I hope they're right. With all my heart, I hope so. But the water's boiling. And not a whole lot of people seem to notice, or care, so far.

Freedom is not "another word for nothing left to lose." And we are letting it go; we are losing it. Freedom requires our steady and passionate devotion. Are we up to that?

A Good Fight

><

This was read at a benefit for the Women's Cancer Resource Center of Berkeley, held at the Palace of Fine Arts in San Francisco on October 23, 1993.

1993

I WAS nine years old at Robin Hood Camp for Girls. Two and a half hours north of Brooklyn, by bus, and mountains and woods and lakes suddenly came together as a real-world situation for me.

I was short for my age, and very young.

It never seemed odd to me that our camp boasted the name of a rather notorious male hero.

I never wondered about the absolute difference between my regular concrete street life in Bedford Stuyvesant and the idyllic circumstance of our summertime cabins and dirt trails and huge, hearty, community meals on the outside deck of the rec hall.

I don't remember puzzling over my experience of seasonal integration, which meant that ten months of the year I lived and played in an entirely Black universe, and then for eight weeks I became a member of a minority of three or four Black girls in a white vacationland of seventy-five to eighty other kids coming from neighborhoods and schools quite different from my own.

I was nine years old and free! I was far away from home, and I was hellbent on having a great time. We played softball and we learned archery and we went on wilderness hikes, overnight, and we burned our tongues on hot chocolate in tin cups and we rode horses, English saddle, and we swam and we made things for our parents in arts & crafts.

I was nine years old and some of the counselors gave me *The Razor's Edge* and *Tender Is the Night* to read after lights out and some of them tried to take away what they called "that filthy rabbit's foot" that my best friend, Jodi, gave me to wear for good luck.

And we sat around campfires and sang under the stars. But best of all, we played softball and I supposed that when I grew up I'd probably become a professional shortstop for some terrific softball team, and then, maybe, after lights out, I'd write my own *Tender Is the Night,* or *Time Must Have a Stop,* or *Magic Mountain.*

Those were my plans. But, in fact, the most exciting thing that happened was that Jodi and I became blood brothers. Of course, it never occurred to us that maybe we should become blood sisters: We were thinking of David and Jonathan when we each cut the inside of our wrists with a penknife and mingled blood to seal our pact of eternal friendship. Not satisfied with that, we formed an elite club, the Dare Devils, and we hammered overlapping capital D's into our silver bracelets that we now could hardly wait to finish in arts & crafts where, formerly, we laconically wove lanyards or beaded belts or painted jewelry boxes for the "old folks" back home.

And, having mingled our blood, and, having hammered our bracelets into distinctive emblems of our bond, our tribe of Dare Devils leaped across big splits in the earth or we set loose the rowboats in the darkness or we swam across the lake, secretly, by moonlight, or we raced each other, on horseback and on foot, and we looked for the highest trees to climb and we played out our days with utmost heart and utmost hilarity and we—nine- and ten-year-old little girls—thought we were young gods fully blessed by all of our lives full of energy and love and an insatiable appetite for danger.

We were daredevils loose on a beautiful planet. We were nine- and ten-year-old little girls and we thought we were free.

Toward the end of that summer, we had a final campfire down by the boats, and the song we sang was, "For all we know—we may never meet again—before you go—make this moment sweet again." We were so young. We could tell that was supposed to be a sad song but we felt no sadness ourselves. We tried not to giggle. We tried to sit in sadness out of respect for the grown-ups sprinkled among us. And I remember wondering if I would sometimes feel sadness, too, when I got old enough to become a counselor.

BUT I WASN'T SURE. Back then I could not imagine the sadness reserved for girls, everywhere.

I would have been amazed by any societal surprise at our Dare Devil/blood brother activities.

I would have been dumbfounded to hear that every fifteen seconds a woman is battered in the United States.

I would never have believed that people kill babies if they're female.

Or that white people despise Black people.

Or that half of all Black mothers have no or inadequate prenatal care.

Or that one out of every eight women in the United States has breast cancer and that before this decade is out, 500,000 American women will die of this disease.

Or that only 5 percent of the money spent for cancer research is spent on finding a cure for breast cancer.

Back then, my ideas of daredeviltry did not conjure up the taking of my Black body into a roadside luncheonette for a forbidden cup of coffee.

I never would have imagined that my loving a white man or that my loving any woman or that my raising my son by my own wits would constitute high risk and certain jeopardy.

And I never would have supposed that the biblical story of Ruth and Naomi held as much heroism, or more, inside its humble womanly narrative as the story of David and Jonathan.

And I would have laughed at anybody who said that someday I'd have breast cancer and that, even after going through a mastectomy, I'd have only a 40 percent chance of survival.

THEN, LAST YEAR, one early morning, there was my friend, Dr. Allen Steinbach, bending over me in the recovery room at Alta Bates Hospital, and Allen was saying, "There's bad news!"

I thought, immediately, that he must mean something godawful had happened to my son, or to one of my friends, but he meant there was bad news for me. They'd performed a biopsy and found an enormous amount of cancer in my right breast.

And so I became one of the millions of American women who must redefine courage and who must redefine the meaning of heroic friendship if we will survive.

And my son and my lover and my friends gathered around like Dare Devils daring themselves and their devotion and their walking of my dog and their changing of the dressing and their seamless and hilarious system of around-the-clock support to save my morale and to save my life.

And it was not easy. And it was not brief. And it is not over.

In between surgery number three and number four, I wrote this poem:

The breath continues but the breathing hurts
Is this the way death wins its way
against all longing
and incendiary thrust from grief?
Head falls
Hands crawl
and pain becomes the only keeper
of my time

I am not held
I do not hold
And touch degenerates into new
agony

I feel
the healing of cut muscle/
broken nerves
as I return to hot and cold
sensations
of a body tortured by the flight
of feeling/normal
registrations of repulsion
or delight

On this meridian of failure or recovery
I move
or stop respectful
of each day
but silent now
and slow

I swear to you I never ever expected to write anything like that, my whole life, but I had to try to tell that truth.

The Women's Cancer Resource Center of Berkeley and the National Black Women's Health Network and Dr. Craig Henderson and Dr. Susan Love and Dr. Denise Rogers and Christopher and Angela and Adrienne and Dianne and Stephanie and Martha and Haruko and Amy and Sara and Pratibha and Lauren and Roberta and Camille and my colleagues and students at school and the neighbors next door and Amigo, the Airedale who lives with me—they dared me to make this cancer thing into a fight: They dared me to practice trying to lift my arm three or four inches away from my side. They dared me to go ahead and scream and cry but not to die. And so I did not die. But I have faced death. And I know death now.

And in the mornings when I walk out into the garden and I see the ninety-seven-year-old willow tree and the jasmine blooming aromatic and the honeysuckle bulging into the air and Amigo gulping at a bumblebee and a stray bluebird lifting itself in flight above the roof of my little house, I am happy beyond belief.

And when I may join with men and women to end the disease

of breast cancer and the disease of race hatred and the disease of misogyny and the disease of homophobia and the disease of not caring about the victims of ethnic cleansing and the victims of our malignant neglect, I am happy beyond belief.

Because this is a good fight. It feels good to me. And, yes, now I know about sadness but I do not live there, in sadness.

And I am happy beyond belief to be here and to join with you to make things better.

Ruth and Naomi,

David and Jonathan:

One Love

⇥⇤

1994

''ENTREAT ME NOT to leave you or to return from follow-ing you; for where you go I will go, and where you lodge I will lodge; your people shall be my people, and your God my God. Where you die I will die, and there will I be buried. May the Lord do so to me and more also if even death parts me from you'' (Ruth 1:16–17).* From earliest childhood, I remember one or another version of these passionate words. As far as I knew, they were the only memorable, and even startling, thoughts attributed to any woman in the Bible. And, as a little girl, I appropriated the fierce loyalty, and the all-out loving commitment embodied by this passage, as an ideal toward which I could and should eagerly aspire. But the story around those unparalleled declarations remained rather wan, and confused, and confusing, in my mind, until this past summer.

* Biblical quotations are taken from the Revised Standard Version.

Yes, I knew it was a woman named Ruth who had so declared herself to Naomi. But I did not understand why. And, as a child, it was not necessary for me to clearly get the context for their relationship, or even for me to clearly fathom their reasons for knowing each other. What mattered to me was that, finally, somewhere, in that big Holy Book, there were words uttered by somebody female to another somebody female. And, what was most important was that her words matched up to the heroic qualities of the other biblical figures I came to memorize and assimilate inside the pantheon of my young heart.

I distinctly remember, for example, my time at an all-girls camp, Robin Hood, in upstate New York. Whenever any of us decided there was need to ceremoniously remark our friendship, we would invent a secret name for ourselves, such as the Dare Devils, and we would mix blood from the inside of our wrists, thereby becoming "blood brothers." Blood sisters simply would not fly; what would that connote? Where was the precedent for "blood sisters" in any literature, or film, or theater piece? Ruth and Naomi, maybe. But did they ever do anything like stealing into the night in order to set loose all of the rowboats, or taking an increasingly perilous walk through the woods—a walk punctuated by bigger and bigger crevasses over which it was necessary to jump—or else retire, humiliated, as a coward?

And were they sisters? I was never sure. But I was certain about David and Jonathan. I knew that Jonathan had been the son of King Saul. And King Saul frequently rushed into battle against the Philistines. And one of the Philistines was Goliath, that huge freak of a warrior on the wrong side. And young David, as just a slender boy, came and slew the giant Goliath with his slingshot. And the King was much impressed. As were all the rest of the Israelites. But none was more moved by the gallantry and intelligence of David than Jonathan. "Jonathan loved him as his own soul" (1 Sam. 18:1).

And after that victory, King Saul insisted that David come and live in the royal palace. But the women of Israel sang, "Saul has slain his thousands, and David his ten thousands" (1 Sam. 21:11), and the King heard this popular outcry of comparison and he became truly jealous. And from that day forward, he eyed David with malice aforethought and, in every way possible, tried to devise David's death. Again and again the King sent young David into battle, hoping that he would be killed. And, even beyond that, the King schemed for David's execution. But, again, and again, the King's son, Jonathan, raced from the palace to warn his friend David and, thereby, saved his life. And after many battles, and much fight and much flight, finally it was obvious that the Lord was with David and that David was, therefore, invincible. And David prevailed. And when David learned of the eventual war deaths of King Saul and of Jonathan, who loved David "as his own soul," David tore his clothes and raised a lamentation that concludes,

> How are the mighty fallen
> in the midst of the battle!
>
> Jonathan lies slain upon thy high places.
> I am distressed for you, my brother Jonathan;
>   very pleasant have you been to me;
>   your love to me was wonderful,
>   passing the love of women.

> (2 Sam. 1:25–26)

So Jonathan had defied his father for the sake of David. And repeatedly he had rescued David from the nefarious intent of his father, the King, thereby jeopardizing his own, otherwise natural, succession to the throne of Israel. And when the King died, David did not rejoice because the King had been "the Lord's anointed." And when Jonathan died, David did not rejoice because to him, Jonathan's love "was wonderful / passing the love of women." Theirs was great reciprocal love. The dimensions of the interaction between the two men approached the mythical in scale. And the content of their intersecting histories is the very stuff of spectacular movie suspense, climax, and triumph.

This summer I became one of the too many thousands of women who must fight breast cancer. From the surgery to determine whether or not there was a malignancy through the surgery for removal of the malignant tissue (a partial radical mastectomy) and the removal of lymph nodes to determine whether or not the cancer had spread, I suddenly became wholly dependent upon the kindnesses of my friends. I had to depend on my friends for my personal care, for the walking of my dog, for the securement of groceries, for the cooking and serving of food, for the cleaning up of the kitchen and of the house, for transportation to and from the doctors, for the handling of correspondence, and for diplomatic dealing with innumerable phonè calls: for my life.

At different points, you would find an elaborate schedule for every day of every week, sometimes broken into hourly segments. Slotted into each segment of each day you would find the name of one or another or yet another friend—a woman friend. And I felt overwhelmed by the exhaustive, seamlessly graceful, and indispensable caretaking organized by these women. How could I possibly have survived any of the ordeal of this fight, and how could I possibly hope to heal, and defeat this cancer, without the unstinting love given to me?

It was Angela, for example, who read everything published on breast cancer and who drove me to the doctor on the morning when the doctor told me that the cancer had spread to the lymph nodes and that, consequently, he was revising his prognosis from 80 percent likely to survive to 40 percent. It was Angela who drove me away from that terrible news to a neighborhood hairdresser whom she begged to "do something" and who, in fact, created a small fire on the top of my head: an electric orange stripe that she bleached into my hair.

It was Adrienne who washed my back and cleansed the wound and told me there was nothing horrible about that horrible procedure, while she changed the sterile dressing. And it was Adrienne who slept through the nights in a chair next to my hospital bed.

It was Lauren who brought bananas, just perfectly not-quite-ripe. And Stephanie who organized my friends into a computer wizardry of a failproof network.

And it was the other Adrienne who traveled all the way from Santa Cruz to bring lunch and laughter and new anthologies of poetry. And Martha who came from New York.

And it was Camille who came at midnight with medicine when the pain was quite unbearable. And Pratibha who came from London.

And it was Sara who talked me through yet another nightmare of giving blood so that the hospital could run necessary, preop tests. And Phyllis who watered the garden several times a week, on her way to work.

And on and on for several months. And I thought, "This is the love of women. This is the mighty love that is saving my life. And where are the public instances of praise and celebration of this love?"

And I found my Bible and, when I could read again, I looked up the story of Ruth to see if I could make better sense of it now.

And I could. And I did.

"In the days when the judges ruled there was a famine in the land" (Ruth 1:1), and for this reason Naomi and her husband and their two sons left Bethlehem and went to a more promising country, the country of Moab. While they stayed there, Naomi's husband died. Her two sons took to themselves two Moabite wives, Orpah and Ruth. And then Naomi's sons died. And Naomi decided she would return to Bethlehem, since the famine had now ended. And so she arranged to bid her widowed daughters-in-law farewell. And one of them, Orpah, wept, and kissed Naomi, and accepted her counsel: She would stay in Moab. But the other daughter-in-law, Ruth, refused to separate from Naomi, and she said, "Entreat me not to leave you or to return from following you." And when Naomi saw that Ruth could not be dissuaded, she allowed her daughter-in-law to return with her to Bethlehem.

Now when the two women returned there, they could not provide for themselves; neither of them was married; neither of them had a husband to protect and feed and honor her. And it was very hard. But Naomi was not about to give up and perish. Nor was she about to permit Ruth to become prey to wanton depredations, or hunger. Therefore, Naomi conceived of a plan whereby Ruth would become appealing to a wealthy farmer and kinsman. Ruth obeyed Naomi and she succeeded in pleasing the kinsman so that he made her his wife. And then Ruth bore the kinsman, whose name was Boaz, a son. And that son became the joy of Naomi's old age. "Then Naomi took the child and laid him in her bosom, and became his nurse" (Ruth 4:16). And Naomi was no longer without family and shelter. And the son of Ruth and Boaz was Obed. And Obed was the father of Jesse. And Jesse was the father of David. Here ended the Book of Ruth.

At first, I was dismayed. The evident dependency of both Naomi and Ruth upon their menfolk struck me as extreme. It was not as though they had set up house together and/or started up a small subsistence farm that then became an amazing commune for other stranded women. And, really, Ruth had to literally put herself at the very feet of Boaz in order to gain the favors of his attention. And suppose Ruth had not found Boaz attractive, or kind, or fun?

And then I realized I was being obtuse. Ruth and Naomi had made brave choices in a circumstance that allowed them no freedom. And they had chosen to do whatever would allow them to stay together, without undue penury, or censure by the townspeople of Bethlehem. And, yes, they could not ride horses into battle and slay the sources for their grief or slay the enemies of their joy. And, yes, they were neither princes nor kings, but, rather, slaves to a social environment that would not permit them any liberty, any respect, any safety, any assurance, even, of work with the reward of food— unless at least one of them became somebody's wife.

But is it not marvelously true that Ruth's love for Naomi was the equal of Jonathan's great love for David? And is it not wonderfully true that Ruth's love for Naomi surpassed her love of men even as David's love of Jonathan surpassed his love of women?

And is it not fitting that the child of Ruth and Naomi should become the father of the father of David? From Ruth and Naomi through David and Jonathan we possess the fabulous history of one love. And, yes, differences of gender have made for huge differences in the documented public display of their differing but always passionate and virtuous attachments. But it is one love. It is love that supersedes given boundaries of birthright or birthplace or conventions of romance or traditions of loyalty. It is one love that yields to no boundary. It is one love that takes you to its bosom and that saves your life.

And we would be foolish to neglect the cultivation and the celebration of such love within our own heroic and our own quite ordinary passage here, on earth.

GIVE ME TWO
REASONS

✴

1994

DEAR BILL CLINTON:

If you think about what can happen in less than thirty seconds, then a year seems like a real long time. That's about as long as you've been holding title to more power than any other individual on the planet. I know you're a man and not a natural resource or a natural disaster. But you're President of these United States, and that should mean something about safety for those of us who put you in the Oval Office.

Whether earthquake or fire or hurricane or corporate "downsizing" or juries arriving at idiot-incendiary conclusions or affluent and fanatical hatemongers standing tall, the big guy in the big house on Pennsylvania Avenue is supposed to protect us, the people, from harm or, failing that, deliver us from desperation. You're the big guy. That's your job. That's what national security requires: our domestic safety from harm and desperation.

If I remember correctly, most women who voted cast their ballots for you, as did most elderly Americans, most young Americans, most African-Americans, most Mexican-Americans, most Asian-Americans, most Chicanos, and most gay and lesbian Americans. Our de facto coalition of choice gave you the major-league boost you needed to move out of Little Rock, Arkansas. And so, the way I see things, you owe us, the new majority of American citizens, a whole lot—as a matter of reciprocity, if nothing else.

Can you give me two reasons why any one of the original Clinton supporters should vote for you again? Or even speak to you? Can you give me two reasons why I should not call you Spineless Sam or confuse you with George Bush?

Given your track record of equivocation, cowardice, and retreat on one hand, plus active humiliation, appeasement, betrayal, and blustery inertia on the other, why should we—folks who celebrated November 3, 1992—believe anything good can come of you, except, perhaps, by accident?

Your failure begins and continues with your willing coexistence with genocide: your refusal to stop so-called ethnic cleansing and the concomitant mass rape of Muslim women in Bosnia.

Then there are your broken promises—to the Haitian refugees, to pro-choice Americans, to gay and lesbian Americans, and to city dwellers ("inner" or "outer" be damned).

Then there is your eating of the defeat of your anyway heavily diluted proposal for jobs.

There is your silence on American poverty except to blame the victims of federal and state neglect and abandonment.

There is your acquiescence to racist and unconstitutional anti-immigrant uproar and proposed legislation.

There is your beating up on the neediest among us: families that qualify for the miserly assistance our welfare programs use as an excuse to belittle and castigate the poor.

There is your absolute zero performance as regards hungry, homeless Americans, who daily increase in number.

Then there is your savage, gratuitous, and unforgivable insult to law professor Lani Guinier.

And, finally, there was that incredible moment of complacency and insolence when you stood in the pulpit of a Black church and presumed to speak on behalf of Dr. Martin Luther King, Jr. Your arrogance was matched only by your ignorance of Dr. King, who, relentlessly, made it clear that Americans will have to pay billions and billions of dollars in order to reverse this country's pathological, four hundred–plus years of racist impact on Black people living here and dying here.

Yes, I know that more than a year ago, your closest advisors had written, "It's the economy, stupid!" on the wall of your "War Room." But I had voted for you because you had actually said: "We cannot afford to waste a single life."

And I had taken you at your word. But you have failed to keep faith with those of us who wanted to trust you.

And that, Mr. President, is the State of the Union today. We are reeling from unnatural and natural disasters without benefit of the rescue and the relief that follow from true executive commitment to the safety of every single life.

Because you have broken so many promises to so many of us, there was only one "brother" in Los Angeles you could call. Rather than creating a new democratic community of inclusion and justice and mercy, you have surrounded yourself with millionaire white men who remain as completely out of touch with the majority of Americans as you are.

But we, the new majority, we exist. And you will learn, Mr. President, that without us, you will become, for good and for evil, beside the point.

A POWERFUL HATRED

⋺⋲

1994

WHAT A SUNNY DAY! Plum trees in pastel bloom. Jasmine in fragrant flowering display. What I'd like to do is fall asleep listening to Prince, or wake myself up, completely, with the energies of Pearl Jam, or walk my dog for three miles in every direction under that very blue sky above me. But other things are happening.

There is a powerful hatred loose in the world. And everything and everyone we cherish is endangered. And so I would have to be some kind of really nearsighted fool to wallow in what's left of the world that's gorgeous and freely given and natural and sweet and hot and unpredictable and delicate and good for growing things. I'd be a wallowing fool unless I also tried to eliminate, or reduce, that hatred that can take all that we have away from us.

But how should I stage my fight? Who will listen to what I have to say?

Except for those occasions when the media smell a possible

chance to pit Blackfolks against other Blackfolks, when do I get calls asking for my thoughts and opinions about anything whatsoever? If the media wanted to know what mainstream Blackfolks think and feel about white folks, for example, they would regularly interview the head of the AME (African Methodist Episcopal) Church and chairs of African-American Studies Departments and a representative sampling of Black students at your nearest high school, and Black writers and thinkers such as Adolph Reed and Angela Davis and Manning Marable and Cornel West and bell hooks.

And what the media would discover is that whether they're looking at somebody separatist or not, most Blackfolks are very clear about one thing: who endangers their lives. Most Blackfolks know he is a powerful white man, such as the President or the Governor or the distinguished U.S. Senator from almost anywhere. And that's how most of us feel most of the time about white men: that they are powerful and dangerous.

And we are not racist. We simply do not have power; white men do. And they—and the few Black men invited in, such as Clarence Thomas, Colin Powell, and Shelby Steele—use that power in ways that cause us enormous harm.

For two decades, federal and state policies have combined to ensure a statistical tragedy of huge magnitude now unfolding in the national Black community. Whether we use indices of unemployment or homelessness or drug addiction or domestic violence or levels of education never attained or official designation as a family on or below the poverty line, our people face a future deformed by boastful government neglect and by hysterical moves to further criminalize and further incarcerate greater and greater numbers of our young men and women. And our people face an uninhibited scapegoat campaign to stigmatize and invalidate the neediest among us: welfare families dependent on AFDC support that amounts to an average of $370 a month for a mother and her two children.

Is it not hateful to equate "crime" and "welfare" with "Black"? That is the equation promoted by Bill Clinton and Pete Wilson, both of them white men who never tire of blathering about these issues they deliberately distort.

• • •

AS THE PRESIDENT tells it, welfare dependency (Black) is a first-priority problem to be eliminated for the sake of good character and the budget. He mouths these sentiments despite the fact that the total percentage of our national budget available for welfare assistance is less than one half of 1 percent. (And, incidentally, most recipients of welfare aid are white, not Black.)

But Bill Clinton knows nothing about good character; good character doesn't follow from working a nine-to-five shift, as he suggests. Good character has to do with honesty and reliability and kindliness.

Clinton and other powerful white men impugn the character of (Black) women on welfare, but where did these men get the idea that raising children is something other than full-time, supremely important, hard work? And exactly what kind of "workfare" are they talking about for single mothers when even white male college graduates cannot find employment? What kind of workfare do they have in mind besides some hideous update of legalized slave labor?

Then there is "crime," which means, according to Clinton and his powerful white cohorts, young Black men. Well, it seems that the Almighty Budget will not tolerate help for the poor, and the Almighty Budget has no money for job creation or for rescue and revitalization of our public schools or for drug rehabilitation or for development and implementation of effective, grassroots community planning, or for social and psychological counseling: No funds available in the Almighty Budget!

But, hey! Bill has a plan: three strikes and you're out forever. And what will that cost California, alone, every year? More than $6 billion! And so, suddenly never mind about the budget. To punish/derogate/imprison/destroy, there are multibillions of dollars in hand, evidently. But to salvage/teach/train/enlighten/empower? No money in the bank!

Now, if you jail somebody at age twenty-five and sentence him to life, that will cost—supposing he lives another forty years—$1 million ($25,000 a year times forty years). So Bill Clinton and Pete

Wilson have $1 million per Black man to spend and it's the God's truth that they're putting that kind of money into his imprisonment, his $25,000-a-year retirement from society.

THERE IS a powerful hatred loose in the world. And most Blackfolks know it. Most of us know it's white, not Black. It's white, not Jewish. It's white and it's male, not female. It's white and it's male and it's heterosexual, not gay or lesbian. We who are weak make it our business to figure out who's strong—strong enough to help us or to crush our lives.

And so we pay attention to truly powerful white men. We notice that the guys who worship at the altar of Pentagon priorities (at a time when the former Soviet Union would not be able to muster a credible threat to Grenada) and who dump all over our human needs in the name of reducing the deficit are the very same guys who think up obscenities like how about taxing food stamps or what about three strikes and you're gone even from the potential for a useful, self-respecting life.

We notice that these are the same guys eagerly collaborating with racist wannabe gatekeepers to America; powerful white men whose ancestors for sure never asked permission to come to this country but just came hell-bent on owning slaves, exterminating Native Americans, and grabbing gold. These powerful white men now conspire to stop immigration to America by anybody who does not resemble themselves. These same powerful white men are the ones who waffle on or ignore women's issues and who betray and/or attack gay and lesbian Americans. These same powerful white men are the ones who will not broach the subject of education except to propose and/or execute additional cutbacks of funds accompanied by the jacking up of student tuition.

These same powerful white men apparently manage to sleep very well at night, thank you, even though their verifiable executive decisions mean that we coexist with absolutely documented genocide, a.k.a., ethnic cleansing in former Yugoslavia.

There is a powerful hatred loose in the world. And it's obvious to most Black people that this hatred is based upon a white supremacist ideology that determines domestic and foreign policies alike. We see American inertia vis-à-vis genocide in Bosnia as part of one horrible continuum that guarantees no action/no deliverance/no beautification/no justice/no peace in South Central L.A. And that continuum is controlled by a white racist value system that does not regard human life as valuable because it's human, because it's alive.

The ruling racist value system of these United States asks three questions of each of us:

1. Does this citizen and his or her group look like somebody I would allow my daughter to marry?

2. Is this citizen and his or her group cheaply available for the enhancement of my profit margins?

3. What can I get away with? In other words, is it "safe" to condemn or ignore or impoverish or imprison or belittle this citizen and his or her group?

THERE IS a powerful hatred loose in the world. And the most powerful practitioners of this hatred do not deploy a hateful rhetoric. They do not declare, "I hate Blackfolks," or "I hate women," or "I hate Jews," or "I hate Muslims," or "I hate homosexuals." They make "civil" pronouncements, such as:

"The Defense Budget must not be cut further"

or "I made every effort to introduce a jobs bill to the Congress but . . ."

or "Top military experts advise against our active intervention in Bosnia"

or "I do not feel comfortable with the writings of my friend, Lani Guinier"

or "The White House is anxious to get past the uproar over gays in the military in order to put its best efforts behind health-care reform"

or "Crime is our number one domestic concern"

or "Illegal aliens threaten to bankrupt state treasuries."

And most Black people notice something else. We notice a virulent, racist double standard. We notice how long we had to wait before the United States adopted any sanctions against South Africa.

We notice that the United States has never even considered sanctions against Israel. We notice that the American media got all excited and riveted by Minister Louis Farrakhan when one of his lieutenants spewed forth loathsome anti-Semitic (and also, by the way, homophobic and misogynist) remarks. We notice that the American media absolutely failed to broadcast or telecast the news of Minister Farrakhan's December 4, 1964, column in *Muhammad Speaks* when he described Malcolm as "a dog returning to its vomit" and when he, Farrakhan, declared that Malcolm was "worthy of death."

Anti-Semitism is wrong. Anti-Semitism is evil. All scapegoating of any kind of people is evil and wrong. Farrakhan and Khalid Abdul Muhammad fulminate about white people, and they trash and vilify that most vulnerable segment of white America: the Jewish population.

I have already turned away from Farrakhan. I was never there. He was never on my side.

Farrakhan runs on hatred. His targets change. But the hatred continues. His views and preachments are not easily distinguishable from those of David Duke. But Farrakhan does not possess a fraction of the power invested in and represented by David Duke.

We notice double standards.

We notice no uproar remotely comparable to the Farrakhan controversy when U.S. Senator Ernest Hollings describes African heads of state as cannibals, or when Jesse Helms utters another unconstitutional commandment, or when Republican Presidential candidate Patrick Buchanan lets loose rabid scattershots against Blackfolks and gay and lesbian Americans and women daring to dream of a life besides and beyond motherhood and vacuum cleaners.

And where were the media and congressional calls for public repudiation of Baruch Goldstein and the rabbi who officiated at his funeral, the rabbi who said, "One million Arabs is not worth a Jewish fingernail," and "We are all Goldstein"?

Why is Baruch Goldstein "a lone, violent madman" and Farrakhan, on the contrary, Public Enemy Number One?

We notice double standards. And we do not like what we see. We do not like what that means. And so, yes, there is fury and there is rage in Black America today. For all of these two decades of terrible reasons, there is Black fury and there is Black rage.

Today the Black community is victim to a national scapegoat campaign that promises to wreck our prospects as a people, irreversibly. And Farrakhan is a distraction, a calculated media distraction of our energies from the real deal: the power of white supremacist ideology here, and everywhere.

Is it conceivable that the media could open up to other Black voices concerned by issues such as government responsibility and equality and justice and building political coalitions and exposing truly powerful white men such as Clinton and Wilson as ambassadors of programmatic hate?

I think it's inconceivable because American media uphold a racist agenda alongside Bill and Pete and Tom and Dick and Harry.

The media construct of Minister Farrakhan leads progressive white Americans and even some Americans of color to believe that the problem is Black racism when, actually, the problem is racism and hatred of any color or kind. And the problem behind that is the problem of who has the power to make whose lives miserable or whose lives over or whose lives fresh and hopeful again.

THERE IS a powerful hatred loose in the world. And there is a savagery of racist double standard ruling our lives. And the way to escape this horror of powerful hatred is to get serious and real clear.

What powerful white man, what powerful white Christian male heterosexual in America today will raise up the model of his lifework as an example opposite to that of Baruch Goldstein, Louis Farrakhan, Bill Clinton, Pete Wilson?

Where can we find a value system seeking to make rather than break connections among our various, frail lives? Where can we find such values invested in any man or woman wielding great political and/or corporate power?

When will we extirpate self-hatred as well as our hatred of folks weaker than we are from our own personal days and nights?

And what is to be done about the really big deal? The President? The governors? The U.S. Senator from almost anywhere? And you and you—whoever you are—perilously interposed between Sarajevo and South Central L.A., what are you going to do?

Injustice and contempt breed hatred.

Hatred reaps hatred.

WE NEED, each of us, to begin the awesome, difficult work of love: loving ourselves so that we become able to love other people without fear so that we can become powerful enough to enlarge the circle of our trust and our common striving for a safe, sunny afternoon near to flowering trees and under a very blue sky.

WE ARE ALL REFUGEES

⊃⊂

1994

THIS IS a moment of enormous and demanding contradiction. In South Africa, Nelson Mandela has become the President of the country that held him in prison for more than twenty-seven years. In South Africa, the new Bill of Rights prohibits discrimination against anyone on the basis of race or gender or class or age or sexual orientation. In South Africa, where 5 percent of the population controls 88 percent of the national wealth, President Mandela has appointed a cabinet committed to a five-year plan carrying forward three key proposals: the construction of one million new homes, a vast public-sector employment program, and universal, free, compulsory education.

In South Africa, where for more than 350 years white racist ideology has enjoyed enforcement by tyrannies of the law and the whip and the bullet, the first democratically elected president, Nelson Mandela, has pledged himself to *nonracial* principles of justice and equal citizen entitlements for all.

Meanwhile, in these United States, where common nouns such as democracy and liberty have long known bumper-sticker popularity, the notion of a Black man or a woman becoming the President remains a joke/a dopey idea/a theoretical construct of small or no plausibility.

In these United States it is difficult to find executive respect for any principle whatsoever except the principle of leadership by following the polls, and that other, most lamentable principle of allocating the least to those in greatest desperation.

Rather than living in a sovereign state in which someone wrongfully imprisoned may nevertheless rise above injustice and one day occupy the highest office, we suffer from budget policies that crush public education up against our ill-considered rush to criminalize and incarcerate and stigmatize and impoverish and deport those men, women, and children among us who possess the most meager array of options.

Rather than the "new world" invoked by President Mandela, our politicians and their media flunkies in these United States spout disinformation designed to bring about an Old World faithful to a Eurocentric, patriarchal history that drags a pretty poor track record into view.

And so you will not hear White House or Sacramento declarations of a five-year plan to meet basic human requirements for housing and employment and knowledge. Instead you will hear White House and Sacramento presentations of a racist slant on public issues of crime, drugs, and so-called welfare, and so-called illegal aliens. Rather than "child care," you will hear "border patrol." Rather than "rehabilitate," you will hear "three strikes and you're out."

And in the absence of a civilizing humane leadership, and in the presence of a leader who contemplates taxation of food stamps, and in the presence of a leader who can betray his promise to Haitian refugees and who can sleep very well in verified coexistence with genocide in Bosnia and who can desecrate the legacy of Dr. Martin Luther King, Jr., by daring to misrepresent Dr. King's analysis, which, contrary to Clinton's galling and appalling assertions, in fact called for billions of dollars to be invested in human salvation undertakings inside South Central L.A. and inside every other city of these United States—in the quandary of such terrible leadership absence and such awful leadership presence, is it any wonder that a ten-year-old boy recently assisted his fourteen-year-old buddy in the killing of a woman for eighty dollars and the hell of it?

In a country where Dan Quayle is reportedly making a comeback no doubt related to the victory of Richard Nixon's burial of Tricky Dick's real life, is it any wonder that the ten-year-old willing accomplice to murder could say something so stupid as: "It wasn't supposed to be like that. It was a game, right?"

And then there is the forgotten issue of the woman. Elizabeth Alvarez, who was the mother of three children and married and now she's dead and the *New York Times* devoted a whole page and a half to her killers: What "the boys" said or didn't say, and what various experts think or do not think about "the boys" and all you ever know about Elizabeth Alvarez is that she was pregnant, she was married, and she's dead.

But how old was she? How come she didn't kill anybody? Did she ever dream or do anything besides get married and have children? Why does the *New York Times* refer to her simply as "a mother of three"? Was she *never* anybody's sister/friend/teacher/confidante/employee/partner or somebody's dearest person in the whole wide world?

I want to know how come Elizabeth Alvarez never ever killed anybody. I want to know how come boys and men commit 87 percent of all violent crimes. And no, I don't think Elizabeth Alvarez is dead because the two killer boys were raised by "women on welfare." But I do think that the fact that the father of one boy abandoned him and his fourteen-year-old mother, and I do think that the fact that the father of the second boy regularly beat up that boy's mother—I do think that these misogynist facts of paternal irresponsibility and violence led to their fatal choice of "a mother of three" as victim.

• • •

AS I THINK about the stories of women—from my students all the way back to my maternal grandmother—again and again I am struck by qualities of hesitation and restraint. Some might interpret these characteristics as facets of mere modesty. But I would disagree. Modesty is something calculated or fake. And it leads nowhere except to the lowering of your eyes. But hesitation and restraint make tenderness and generosity and altruistic interaction possible and even likely.

Hesitation and restraint quiver quietly alive someplace opposite to violence and domination. And I wonder about that apparently unequal equation.

Is that the problem, worldwide?

Is the female of the species some kind of noble/virtuous setup for her male counterpart?

How come Elizabeth Alvarez never killed anybody?

If she ever imagined boy-killers under development and wanted to evade a violent death, where could she go? Where could she find sanctuary?

As a woman, married or not, and pregnant or not, and mother of one/two/three, or none—where could she find political or economic asylum that would mean safety and respect and equal access to freedom *and to the power* to guarantee her own safety and her own equal access to freedom?

Instead of Mandela's New World, our politicians and their media flunkies busily and viciously strive to resurrect an Old World in which there will be no safety, no asylum, for anybody but themselves. These men, direct descendants of other men who came to America never asking anybody's permission to arrive or to invade or to conquer or to exterminate or to enslave or to betray or to exploit and discriminate against those who preceded them and those who, willingly or not, came after them—these men now contrive a so-called immigration crisis and they invent and then promulgate pathological idiot terms like "illegal aliens."

But, as a matter of fact, the planet is not entirely white, or male. And the United States is no longer mostly white, and it will never be more than 50 percent male. And today's wannabe gatekeepers are having themselves a holy-cow fit about this in-your-face situation of their inevitable decline. And so they castigate every one of the varieties of colored peoples seeking entry into our beloved American experiment of a multiracial/multiethnic/multicultural body politic. And, as usual, the punishing burden of this hateful effort to exclude and to reject people clamoring for refuge and relief, the brunt of this hatred falls upon the weak: Eighty percent of the 100 million displaced people on the planet are women and children—80 percent! Overwhelmingly, the face of displaced humanity is a female face. Overwhelmingly, her female predicament of multifaceted oppression remains not recognized as a political predicament. And, so, overwhelmingly, most refugees do not qualify for political asylum.

But what if we women everywhere arose to demand political asylum from the personal and the institutional violence and domination that scar our existence everywhere? What if we demanded political asylum for ourselves—on the job, on the block where we live, in the bedrooms where we want to find and make love?

What if we declared ourselves *perpetual refugees* in solidarity with all refugees needing safe human harbor from violence and domination and injustice and inequality?

Could we arise with characteristic hesitation and restraint and nevertheless be seen, be heard, be strong enough to change our homes, change our streets, change our immigration policies, change our total national states into political and economic asylum for ourselves—the majority of human life?

In this American space disfigured by traditions of hatred and selfishness, we are all alien and we are, none of us, legitimate.

We are all refugees horribly displaced from a benign and welcoming community.

And the question is: Can we soon enough create the asylum our lives will certainly wither without?

Well, I behold the miracle of Mandela. And I behold the equally improbable miracle of domestic and international women's groups creating power out of sorrow and away from pain. I look at the Women's Foundation, and the National Black Women's Health Project, and the National Asian Women's Health Organization, and the California Abortion and Reproductive Rights Action League finding out the facts, fighting for our dignified, fearless, and happily consequential female freedom, and to me the answer is easy, it's obvious. We're doing it!

O. J. SIMPSON: INNOCENT

OF WHAT?

ⰌⰌ

1994

THE NIGHT of the two "brutal murders" (what do they mean by "brutal"? Is there some other kind?), I drove my Rolls-Royce to McDonald's and, just like that, I got something to eat. I have a witness! He rode with me, this (white) guy who lives in my guest house on my $2 million property in Los Angeles. Driving the Rolls for two Big Macs, a double order of fries, and a large strawberry shake—all for myself—well! The way I see it, I already won my case.

Like I said, many times, I never wanted anybody to see me as a Black man. I wanted to be different, to be more than that: a bona-fide mega-rich and famous star.

Didn't I run 2,003 yards on a football field in 1973? Okay, that was a while ago. Okay, I never particularly tried to protect somebody weaker than me. And I never took on people very much bigger or more powerful than me. But, so what? Folks call me a hero because of the way I ran with the ball. They called me a hero and I was having a pretty good time.

Okay, back in 1968, my first wife—she was Black—she *is* Black—she told some magazine, I think it was *Look* magazine, that I was "a beast" and "pretty horrible." But that was her slant on things.

I was having a pretty good time. As a matter of fact, she was pregnant with our third child when I saw this eighteen-year-old-fresh-outta-high-school-like-to-blow-me-away. She was so beautiful! So there was my first (Black) wife pregnant with our third child and then I meet this girl and she's white and blond and perfect and everything and I went crazy for her and I was this big-time hero and so I started seeing her (the white girl) and ended up making her my second wife. I was having a pretty good time.

And that girl, well, she was my wife for more than fifteen years, you know, and she'd always bring me breakfast in bed—every damn day!—and she never did stop looking good to me. And that's kind of a long marriage as these things go. But, then, you watch those Black women out here going off about how the white girl was my "problem"—my "downfall," you know—and I'm supposed to be this "Brother" victimized by yellow hair and blue eyes. Can you believe it? I was having a pretty good time.

As a matter of fact, in the two years since my second wife and I got divorced, I've been "victimized," again, by another real beautiful, young white woman I've been dating steadily. I *am* having a pretty good time!

In the newspapers today, they said, "The O.J. of Old Returns: Confident in Court. He smiles and gives thumbs up to his supporters." They said I was "nattily attired." Stuff like that. I'm big! I'm telling you! I already won my case. The papers note that I didn't even "acknowledge" the families of "the victims" (my—white—wife and her friend). But they leave it right there! Nobody's asking how come I wouldn't want to say, "I'm sorry, too," or "I'm grieving, too," or things along that line to the family of my brutally murdered (white) ex-wife—unless I'm not sorry or grieving or whatever. But nobody's bringing that up! No! They concentrate on the fact that I "look like a winner."

Hell, I *am* a winner! If I was a regular Black man, can you imagine the same Los Angeles Police Department that chased down and just about killed Rodney King hanging back, for hours and for miles, while I was riding my Bronco (I left the Rolls-Royce in my garage) with a passport plus $10,000 in cash, trying to figure out what I want to do or where I want to go? Can you imagine that? Hah!

Now Rodney King—he was and is a regular Black man. But me? I'm a winner. I had those turkeys talking all kinds of Mr. This and Mr. That. I'm big, I'm telling you! I'm having a pretty good time!

I got three of the baddest and most expensive (and white) attorneys in the whole United States day and night defending my butt. As a matter of fact, we just decided (okay, belatedly) to add on a Black lawyer for the image thing, plus local L.A. public relations, and so forth. But I'm paying for this! I have that kind of Rolls-Royce bread to burn.

It's like this clown said a couple weeks ago: "Celebrity creates its own color, its own class, and its own laws." I'm here to tell you, that's the truth! I'm so rich and I'm so famous that ABC-TV gave me way more coverage than they gave to Nelson Mandela when he took over South Africa. You ready for that? And more than they ever thought about giving to Ron Dellums, who's been kicking ass in Congress for twenty-some years. And way, way more than they gave to the President's State of the Union. I'm not lying to you. You see what I'm saying? I've already won!

But there are these other women carrying on about "domestic violence." And sometimes that garbage gets on my nerves pretty bad. It's no big deal: Like I've said, many times, it's a family matter.

But these other women march around with these numbers about a domestic violence death every day and a half in L.A. County, where I happen to live, and four million women battered every year, one every five seconds, and 80 percent of wives and girlfriends needing rescue turned away because there are only 1,500 shelters in the USA and sixty beds in all of San Francisco and you can choke your wife into unconsciousness and/or beat her bloody and break her arm or her leg or her nose and the law calls that a misdemeanor and I swear! Sometimes this garbage gets on my nerves! Like the nine times in 1989 when my ex-wife (the white one) called the cops because I got pretty damn mad about something and so I beat her up so she'd listen to me better. And that other time in 1993 when she told them I was going to kill her and now she's dead and it's goddamn annoying, sometimes, this "domestic violence" bullshit!

But I'm having a pretty good time! At first I was kind of depressed. But I got over that. And folks are buying and selling these T-shirts dedicated to me. And I don't have to do anything I don't feel like doing. I don't have to say "Boo!" or "Diddley-Squat" to my (white) ex-wife's family, or anybody. So long as I show up "nattily attired," and "smiling," and "thumbs up," I'm a winner!

And besides me, you ever heard of a Black man who could pick and choose when he was a Black man? You see what I'm saying? I'm different! I made it! I'm not a Black man! Just like I always wanted! I'm big! I'm a star! I'm having a pretty good time!

AN ANGRY BLACK WOMAN
ON THE SUBJECT OF THE
ANGRY WHITE MAN

>⊱⊰<

Dedicated to the Negro U.C. Regent, Ward Connerly, who gave more than
$100,000 to the campaign of Governor Pete Wilson and who led the U.C. Regent
attack on Affirmative Action, 1995.

1995

We didn't always need affirmative action
when we broke this crazy land into farms
when we planted and harvested the crops
when we dug into the earth for water
when we carried that water into the big house kitchens and
    bedrooms
when we fed and clothed other people's children with the
    food we cooked and served to
other people's children wearing the garments that we fitted
    and we sewed together,
when we hacked and hauled huge trees for lumber and fuel,
    when we washed and
polished the chandeliers

when we bleached and pressed linens purchased by the dollar
  blood profits from our
daily forced laborings
when we lived under the whip and in between the coffle and
  chains
when we watched our babies sold away from us
when we lost our men to anybody's highest bidder
when slavery defined our days and our prayers and our
  nighttimes of no rest
—then we did not need affirmative action.
Like two-legged livestock we cost the bossman three hundred
  and fifteen dollars or six
hundred and seventy-five dollars and so he provided for our
  keep
like two-legged livestock
penned into the parched periphery of very grand plantation
  life
we did not need affirmative action. No! We needed overthrow
  and a holy fire to purify
the air.
And so we finally got freedom on a piece of paper.
But for two hundred years in this crazy land the law and the
  bullets behind the law
continued to affirm
the gospel of God-given white supremacy
For two hundred years the law and the bullets
behind the law and the money and the politics behind that
  money behind the bullets
behind the law affirmed the gospel of God-given white
  supremacy God-given male
white supremacy.

And neither the Emancipation Proclamation nor the Civil War nor
one constitutional amendment after another one nor one civil rights
legislation after another could bring about a yielding of the followers

of that gospel to the beauty of our human face. Justice don't mean
nothin' to a hateful heart!

And so we needed affirmative action. We needed a way into
the big house
besides the back door. We needed a chance at the classroom
and the jobs and open
housing
in okay neighborhoods
We need a way around the hateful heart of America
We needed more than "freedom" because a piece of paper
ain't the same as opportunity or
education.
And so thirty years ago we agitated
and we agitated until the President declared,
"I now decree our federal commitment
to equality not
just as a right
but to equality
in fact"
and a great rejoicing rose like a spirit
dancing
fresh and happy on the soon-to-be-integrated-
and-most-uppity ballroom floor
of these United States.
And Blackfolks everywhere dressed up in African-
American pride
and optimism
from the littlest to the elders
we shined our shoes and brushed our hair
and got good and ready
for "equality in fact"
But (three decades later) and come to find out
we never got invited to the party
we never got included in "the people"

we never got no kind of affirmative action worth
more than spit in the wind
unless somebody real articulate can up and explain to me
how come (in 1997)
39.9 percent of Black children living in poverty
and in 1993
the net worth of African-Americans averages
$4,418 compared to $45,740 for whites
and don't get me started
about the cities / the federal
and state evisceration of our public
schools / the federal and state
investment in prisons and cops
and prisons and cops
because then maybe I won't be able to stop
myself
from going on and going off

and yesterday
the new man in the White House
the new President
he said, "What we have done for women and minorities is a
    very good thing, but we
must respond to those who feel discriminated against. . . .
    This is a psychologically difficult
time for the so-called angry white man."

Well I am here to tell the world that 46 percent of my
    children living in poverty
don't feel good to me
and more Black men in prison cells than college
don't feel good to me
psychologically
or otherwise!

Tell that angry white man "Get a grip!"

White men constitute 44 percent of the American labor force
    but white men occupy 95 percent
of all senior management positions!

And 80 percent of the congress, four fifths of tenured
    university faculty, nine tenths of the United States
Senate—and 92 percent of the Forbes 400!

Hey guys, get a grip!
You say you're angry?
Who's angry?!!!

I say the problem with affirmative action seems to me like
way too much affirmative talk
but way too little action!

WHERE I LIVE NOW

❧

1995

LESS THAN a month ago, somebody wrote this on a wall at Fairfield University in Connecticut. "Fuck unity, you minorities. The white race is superior. I think we should hang all Blacks, chinks, and spics. Let's unite and form a new generation of KKK. To all my white brothers and sisters, let's take over what once was ours. Minorities just cause problems, and we don't need them. All Blacks should go to Africa, all chinks should go to hell, and all spics should get on their banana boats and go back to their island. If by 10:30 A.M. all minorities don't leave F.U., me and my fellow brothers will start killing and raping minority bitches."

A few days before this message (signed by "the KKK" and adorned by several swastikas), the *New York Times* committed the unnatural full weight of its Book Review to various popular exercises in behalf of white supremacy.

The next weekend, when I was speaking in Lexington, Kentucky, a white policeman there shot an unarmed eighteen-year-old Black teenager in the head, and killed him.

I had arrived in Fairfield, Connecticut, barely twenty-four hours after California, the most populous and the largest and the most heterogeneous state of this Republic, reelected Pete Wilson.

As governor, Wilson has accomplished quite a lot. He has established the bizarre notion of an "illegal alien" in the respectable discourse about the issue of immigration to this country, which is a country of Native Americans, African-Americans, and—everybody else, for damn sure—immigrants, or, in the case of Mexican-Americans/Chicanos, forcibly displaced indigenous peoples.

He has further poisoned public debate through the deployment of TV commercials that depict Mexicans as crazed roaches swarming over and through and around defenseless toll booths and paralyzed highway traffic.

He has espoused "three strikes and you're out" and now, with the passage of Proposition 184, that amazing idea has become a law meaning that, within ten years, California will spend 2.5 times more money on prisons than it will spend on education. (Incidentally, at the rate of at least $25,000 a year, the cost of lifetime imprisonment—assuming forty years—is one million bucks.)

And, consistent with his "illegal alien" hysteria, Proposition 187, another new law in California, means that anyone who appears "suspicious" shall be reported to authorities and denied classroom/emergency room entry. Presumably I will be wasting my time if I report anybody who looks like Pete Wilson: White is not "suspect." And, of course, white is smart—very smart. In fact, only those suspicious-looking Asian-Americans tend to defeat white folks at their own game: that same old Stanford-Binet blah-blah that excuses me from my life, really, because, given my genetic deficiency, what can you expect of me, anyhow?

So I arrived in Fairfield, Connecticut, feeling pretty low. My host, a young white senior from Nashua, New Hampshire, Paul Kelley, handed me a copy of the KKK ultimatum to read, once I climbed into his four-by-four. But it was hard to concentrate. Besides the heavy rain outside, Paul was telling me the whole deal of

Aryan recruitment on the nearby beaches and anti-Semitism on campus and homophobic attacks, and I was wondering if I had really flown across the entire USA or was I just turning around and around in one spot: where I live now.

The same experts who think I'm stupid believe that (c.f., *The Handmaid's Tale*) white women of the right genetic composition should be breeding more or that only such women should have babies—regardless of the wishes of these genetic superstars—if "the decline" or "the elevation" of "the intelligence" of "the race" is at stake. And, conversely, one Mississippi politician ran for office by showing a poster of a Black woman and her child: A vote for him was a vote against such an affront to eugenic considerations.

I was looking at the students: Asian- and African- and Hispanic- and Native American and white and mostly Catholic and mostly female. It was a small gathering in a small room. But the fact of our common jeopardy was palpable, and as I listened to their modest demands for safety and representation, I felt almost calm: They were working it out. They had to.

None of these facts had changed: The KKK had not been captured or extirpated from their lives. Curricular inclusion of anything resembling multicultural studies was years away. But a fifth of the student population had joined a demonstration against hatred. (Not nothing, but not a majority response, either.)

Back home, it took a while to get the stats. And when I heard the news, I was dumbfounded: 57 percent of Asian-Americans, and 50 percent of African-Americans, and 30 percent of Latinos had voted for Proposition 187. Talk about critical ignorance and/or horribly successful disinformation!

Where I live now is the same place where, during the 1920s, an involuntary sterilization plan was conceived and implemented. In the 1930s, the Nazis based their forced sterilization policies on the California model.

Where I live now is on the Western side of the Rockies. On the other side, my son was riding his bike from the University of Colorado–Boulder Law School library when a car full of white men tried to run him off the road as they made obscene suggestions about what he should do with himself. Boulder is where there are no Indians around but you do have a mania for 1 percent body fat, no smoking, and, also, threatening phone calls to a young Jewish couple who moved there, recently, and whose car has been vandalized.

Over here, in Berkeley, certain Americans approach other Americans in the supermarket or on the sidewalks asking "the other" Americans if they're in the United States legally, or not, and if they can prove whatever they say.

Where I live now makes me wonder if Nazi Germany's night skies ever beheld a really big moon—a heavenly light that failed to dispel the cold and the bitter winds tormenting the darkness of earth below.

Where I live now there is just such a moon tonight—a useless, huge light above our perishing reasons for hope.

WHERE I LIVE NOW,

PART TWO

><

1995

ALREADY, NOVEMBER 1994 feels far away. That was a seriously bad moment. And many of us lost morale because we accepted mass media reports of a Republican "sweep" or a Republican "revolution." And so we thought we were doomed inside the tightening jaws of racist jeopardy, or worse. We were surrounded by enemies. We were few. We were weak. We had been slammed into the realm of the irrelevant.

It took a little while before we reexamined the arithmetic pertinent to those elections: If only 39 percent of the electorate cast a ballot, and if only 19 percent of the electorate voted Republican, then where was this mythical "landslide," exactly? What was the source for claims of a "monumental mandate"?

To be sure, the majority of the minority of Americans who did vote opted for the ignorant, mean, and self-destructive side of the choices available. And with Newt Gingrich chasing giraffes when he's not racing after more and more personal power, and with Bill Clinton as the redoubtable alternative to leadership of any kind, things in Washington continue to look dangerous and dismal—indeed, like a man-made disaster.

But I have been watching the Japanese response to the natural disaster of a 7.2-point earthquake that has taken the lives of more than 5,000 people, catapulted more than 300,000 into homelessness, and lifted bottom-line attributes into tragic and awe-inspiring relief. Throughout the wrecked cities of Kobe and Osaka, we have witnessed pervasive displays of dignity and communal concern despite ultimate stress. There has been no violence inside that critical context of no water, no blankets, no food. There has been no looting. We have seen a massive loss of life but no loss of civil humanity.

As a matter of fact, citizens of Japan donated $2,450,000 in rescue monies for the California Bay Area, following our 1989 Loma Prieta earthquake, which was horrifying and deadly and, also, a fraction of the fatal force of the Kobe-Osaka ordeal. But are we talking "Japanese" here? Are these the people regularly maligned by the American mass media as "ruthless" and "techno-robots" addicted to "incomprehensible conformity"?

I notice that the elected officials of Japan have not distinguished themselves—through words or deeds—in this hour of devastating and inarguable human need. I notice that this absence of "leadership" has not impaired the resilient and noble spirit of the ordinary men and women who have survived.

Evidently, we belong to a species capable of individual initiative and virtue beyond self-serving ambition and desire.

In the absence of human authority and regulation, for example, we can choose to preserve or to salvage a civil community.

This is pretty big, pretty good, news.

TEN DAYS BEFORE the Kobe-Osaka earthquake, I spent a week in Heartland America. God knows I was not eager to go there. Given the American mass media portrayals of the prairie as grounds for extreme provincialism, white/right-wing Christianity, and die-hard zealotry for the never-never-world of "the way things were," I dreaded my trip as a possibly foolish foray into hostile and unfamiliar turf.

Subsequently, I learned that mass media projections of my people and my culture had induced corresponding dread among some of my would-be hosts at Mankato State University in Minnesota. Furthermore, the anger that drives some of my published writings had predisposed them to perceive me as negative, narrow, and bigoted—and/or "irrational."

Well, Mankato is about seventy-five miles southwest of the Twin Cities. It is certainly white. It's cold. It's a hard place to live. It's mostly Swedish and Lutheran. The average height of a young white man, out there, is six foot one. Most everybody eats beef and cheese. And above that town of 42,000 residents, you see an enormous stretch of open sky.

From day one of my arrival, I was met with generosity and kindness plus the intellectual courtesy of my hosts, who had bothered to read and wrestle with my works beforehand. During my stay as a scholar-in-residence, there were several occasions when interested faculty and students shot questions at me or declared their own convictions about, for example, public education, or domestic violence, or problems of diversity, or curtailment of police power, or feminism, or urban planning, or the use of knowledge.

Very quickly, I recognized my environment as welcoming, in the best sense. We did not want to agree or disagree, but we were trying to speak to each other across high barriers of misinformation and visceral response to obvious, and very significant, differences.

In any case, it was not that cold. And it was not that white. The president of the Mankato State Student Association is an extremely persuasive young Black man, Kris Hammes. In the highest echelons of the administration, there are two Black men, Lewis Jones and Mike Fagin, who enjoy unqualified respect. I twice visited a class in multicultural literature led by a Native American, Gwen Griffin. This is the point: The Heartland is no alien enclave, no haven for mean-spirited and ill-informed activity.

When I met with Mankato State honor students, they told me that so many graduates, male and female, hope to become public school teachers there is now an astonishing glut: in one instance, five thousand candidates applied for one opening in a remote school. Mankato inculcates a value system that does not kneel to regular goals of greed and domination.

Above all, I felt safe among these strangers. There is a Minnesota code of honor that reflects their annual battle with sub-zero temperatures and sudden, blinding snow. That code requires everybody to stop and provide assistance to anyone who seems to be stuck or stranded, outdoors, in wintertime. To this golden rule, there are no amendments, no exceptions. And this willing commitment leads to a reliable meaning of civil community that, I believe, makes possible their commonplace kindness and generous poise.

In the absence of social and cultural diversity, it is nevertheless possible to seek and to find bonding information and connections with people unlike yourself.

This is pretty big, pretty good, news.

I am not saying anything like "perfect" or "paradise." But in these times of boastful cruelty, racist scapegoating, and a virulent recrudescence of white supremacist activity, in these times of the media's malevolent intervention between peoples, it is heartening to know that, on our humble, fumbling-forward, two feet, we can discover or join or rescue human community. We can secure safety and justice and grace for all of our difficult days together without any leadership—besides our own.

IN THE LAND OF

WHITE SUPREMACY

⋇

1995

I USED TO THINK I was up against racist belief and behavior. But then, about a year ago, I began to focus on white supremacy. Whatever that might mean, I didn't have Aryan Nation–type in mind. I was watching and listening to an everyday, casual kind of mental disorder: something real homespun and regular, like my (white) doctor saying she'd eaten Chinese food twice last week, but the rest of the time, she'd opted for "American."

Or it might be something ordinary like media references to "The Heartland" as "true" America, even though very few of us live in North Dakota, Minnesota, or, for that matter, Oklahoma, and even though the majority of Americans reside on the East or West Coast. And California, for example, is the most populous as well as the most heterogeneous (non-"Heartland") state in the Union.

These were the kinds of things I began to hook up inside my head. I came to recognize media constructions such as "The Heartland" or "Politically Correct" or "The Welfare Queen" or "Illegal Alien" or "Terrorist" or "The Bell Curve" for what they were: multiplying scattershots intended to defend one unifying desire—to establish and preserve white supremacy as our national bottom line.

Racism means rejecting, avoiding, belittling, or despising whatever and whoever differs from your conscious identity.

White supremacy means that God put you on the planet to rule, to dominate, and to occupy the center of the national and international universe—because you're "white."

Anything or anyone appearing to challenge your center-stage position and its privileges becomes ungodly, or the Devil, or the Devil Incarnate, as in "The Jews," "The Niggers," "The Wetbacks," "The Chinks."

White supremacy moves beyond racist formulations of "superior" or "inferior." White supremacy takes hatred of the unfamiliar to the level of religious war between "good" and "evil." Underlying such a world view is an infantile mentality as obviously infantile as it is "normal" in these United States.

And so the catastrophe of the Oklahoma City bombing becomes a possible, and, for some, a reasonable, carefully planned event. Nothing and no one—not a one-year-old baby, not a two-year-old child, not unremarkable American workers going about their boring but useful routines, not mothers or fathers or day-care teachers or any number of the simply living—could interdict or mitigate the murder-crazy determination of white supremacists to declare their hatred of "the government" and their hatred of anyone who fails to mirror their faces set, killer resolute, against us.

It has taken me until the tragedy of Oklahoma City to understand that "The Aryan Nation" is not the name of an organization of some sort. "The Aryan Nation" is the goal of the Christian Coalition and the Patriot Militias and the Contract with America and Governor Pete Wilson. "Come unto me all ye who suffer and who seek asylum and an open road, and I will blow you away! I will efface you from my territory, my Aryan Preserve!"

To impose an Aryan Nation upon these United States would

require bodily and juridical and legislative assault upon the constitutional liberties and the constitutional protection that defines basic citizenship here. But Aryan Nation wannabes feel fine about that because only the godly deserve to be free.

To impose an Aryan Nation upon these United States would require overthrow of our government and that's also okay because, as some of us may remember, it's supposed to be a government of and by and for "the people"—and, at last count, "the people" have begun to look less and less like Clint Eastwood playing an unemployed marine at a Christian revival meeting.

And, besides, the only democratic justification for centralized, federal government is its provision for the security of the population it presumes to represent. But you cannot provide for the security of a people without justice, without equality, without food, without education, without gainful employment, without housing. And so we pay taxes to "the government" expecting that, in return, we will receive these goods fundamental to our personal security and to the security of our society.

Hence, affirmative action, for example, is a federal government policy. Hence, the viciously orchestrated attack on "affirmative" for the sake of "angry white men" who, statistics inform us, continue to occupy 95 percent of all senior management positions.

I guess that was the picture of one of those angry white men, that photograph of blond, white Timothy McVeigh. Is that the guy who bombed the federal office building and killed 167 human beings because something truly pissed him off? Is he one of those guys "affirmative action" irritated like, so to speak, crazy?

And he wasn't really "Middle Eastern–looking," was he? What a shock! He looked "American," one of the sheriffs remarked.

And then there was the President droning on about our task is to cleanse ourselves of this "dark" force.

"Dark," Mr. President?

On the contrary. White. White. American white supremacist white. The monster is an "American-looking" white man. This violent, paramilitary hatred is absolutely homegrown and growing.

Do not be misled. There is no difference between hating "the government" and hating "the Jews" and "the Niggers" in the mind-mesh of the Christian–white rights crusade.

And forget about Negro clowns in the tradition of Clarence Thomas—clowns like the University of California regent Ward Connerly, who has risen to national stature by attacking affirmative action, or the Negro head of a right-wing militia group in Alameda, California. There have always been fools who have flared into infamy almost like an awful amusement before the curtain lifts.

The Oklahoma City bombing has lifted the curtain.

If we do not see ourselves, at last, stripped of all excuse and scapegoat, if we do not recognize the weakness of our connections to other—all of us different, and different-looking Americans—as the wellspring for white supremacy, then we may as well admit that we are ready to submit to Timothy McVeigh's final agenda for our country: to achieve an Aryan Nation by any means necessary.

MY MESS, AND OURS

➤∈

1995

BOOKS AND PAPERS no longer pretended to pile up. Every surface stunned me with too many questions. My house was a mess.

I decided to withdraw. I carried different sections of my personal chaos into my bed. In the space of ten days, I read: "Extracts from Pelican Bay," a nearby maximum-security prison; two books by Kenzaburo Oe; a *Village Voice* exposé of INS "detention" of 82,000 immigrants; a belated report on the enslavement of seventy-two young women and girls, in Los Angeles; several statistical descriptions of America's binge appetite for locking up more than a million other Americans; and daily newspaper accounts of the current U.S. Congress "at work."

Apparently believing that "affirmative action" is the reason why California schools are no longer always or mainly "white," the governor and his friends voted to abolish affirmative action on our nine University of California campuses as an obvious—if equally deluded, and ignorant, and hateful, and doomed—sequel to their invention of Proposition 187.

President Clinton did nothing to rescue the Muslim peoples of Bosnia from "ethnic cleansing." Photographs documented mass graves barely covering the limbs of Muslim men and women. And "the left" agonized about whether or not verified genocide warrants whatever—*whatever action*—will stop it.

Because it was almost the fiftieth "anniversary" of Hiroshima, I began reading, or rereading, Ronald Takaki, John Hersey, and Howard Zinn.

Dizzy with new information about Allied atrocities committed against the civilian peoples of Hamburg and Dresden, as well as American atrocities committed against Tokyo, Kobe, and Osaka, I felt nauseated by the jingo lingo of popular "discussions" blossoming around me.

I could barely lift my head. When I did, I found myself watching, by accident, a television special about hundreds of thousands of female babies abandoned in China, where they endure (for as short a time as they may live) orphanage circumstances. The state keeps these babies tied—by their arms and by their legs—to little chairs that double as latrines.

I got out of bed. I walked to the windows overlooking my street. It was sunny. It was quiet. It was early morning. I began to clean. I picked things up. I threw things out. I alphabetized. I labeled. I put newspaper clippings in green folders. I put business correspondence in a blue folder. Everything connected to my writing went into a red or an orange folder: "poetry," "prison," "race," "family," "women," "children," "violence," "California demographics," "South Africa," "Japan," "Ireland," "Israel," "welfare," "Bosnia," "Los Angeles."

I swept. I mopped. I scrubbed. Now there was the dining room table, after all!

I took books from their shelves and ordered them by type: novels/poetry/current affairs/reference. And then I began to subdivide. To take a break. I Windexed this or that window. I organized the videotapes. I dusted. I brushed my dog.

Exhausted, but very excited, I moved from room to room, sitting down and eyeing, with expectant pride, the flagrant orderliness of my environment.

Nothing was loose or cluttered. Everything looked clean and settled. There was space to my right and to my left and straight ahead: space. Either things fit unobtrusively into that space or they had become invisible. I had put them away. I had eliminated the mess. I had taken control.

AFTER FIVE MINUTES of orderly bliss, I realized I was bored, and rather uncomfortable. I had created fake attributes of fake serenity. If I wanted to do anything whatsoever besides sit around—if I wanted to read or write or fact-check or even make a phone call—I would have to disturb this still-life-by-a-wannabe-housewife situation.

And so it came to me that I am just a very ordinary 1995 American. Maybe what I thought I was doing with my house is what so many Americans think they're doing with the world and with the USA—putting away the problems: locking them up, throwing them out, or pasting stupid labels on really complicated varieties of pain and aspiration so that everybody you don't know, and everybody you don't understand, will fit into a blue or an orange folder that will slide into a blue-only or an orange-only filing cabinet that some security guard will slam shut for the sake of tidy appearances.

My domestic maneuvers establish my credentials for the clean-shirt-to-the-fire brigade. In my madness for "neat" and "clean," I may enter that frightening frontier where folks finally say, "Put it away!"/"Clean them out!"/"Tie her to a chair!"/"Hold him in a six-by-three-foot cell!"

And, then, shall we sit down and admire the space around us: all that still life, all that vanishing connection to our humanity?

JUSTICE AT RISK

⋇

1995

JUST ABOUT every time anybody talks about affirmative action or multicultural education, the presentation seems simple: White Western authorities on beauty and honor and courage and historical accomplishment have denied and denigrated whatever and whoever does not fit into their white Western imagery.

Some people who have been systematically excluded by white Western tradition will never know anything beyond hourly work at minimum wage. Some people will never know anything besides the pain of physical poverty and psychological self-loathing. Some people will never know anything except dependency upon those who despise them, those who create and impose conditions that enforce despicable dependency.

And so, in order to avoid figurative and literal extinction, and in order to provide for self-respecting knowledge, and social mobility based upon such knowledge, we who have been denied and denigrated now undertake to ascertain our own beauty and honor and courage and historical accomplishment according to our own images of truth of our distinctive human being.

All of this seems simple.

But public discussion of affirmative action and multicultural studies has been warped by all kinds of media machinations, as political ambitions and lies and panic and your elementary white supremacy/race hatred erupt. Politicians like California's Governor Pete Wilson and his devoted appointee, U.C. Regent Ward Connerly, become famous, and infamous. And Wilson tries to run toward the White House propelled by the poisonous uproar against affirmative action that he and his cohorts have conspired to ignite in the first place.

Craziness. But it didn't take much and it didn't take long before "affirmative action" became the so-called pivotal issue, nationwide.

White people everywhere agreed to interviews on the subject. Heavyweight presidential prospect Colin Powell, a Black man, actually got points for his "brave" refusal to condemn "affirmative action" categorically.

National media potentates borrowed from Connerly, and "racial preference" quickly eclipsed "affirmative action."

So now the question put to white Americans changed to, "What do you think about job and college-admission policies that give preference to some racial groups over others? Do you think that's fair?"

This double whammy, this model of loaded public inquiry, produced great excitement and front-page news: Gosh, no! White Americans didn't think "racial preference" was really "fair." And, as a matter of fact, once you redefined things like that, a whole lot of Black and Latino and Asian-Americans didn't think "racial preference" was really "fair," either!

Soon our national press exploded with outcries from "angry white men" and a minicascade of first-person white student reports from universities overtaken by unqualified barbarians, politically correct thought police, and apologetic, but terrified, would-be employers who had truly wanted to hire the best white man for the job, but could not.

In July of 1994, the U.C. Regents voted to end affirmative action throughout the University of California system of public education. And I suppose that everyone opposed to "racial preference" breathed easier as the prospect of preserving a mostly white Western curriculum for mostly white Western students who would later lead or join a mostly white labor force brightened a little bit. Obviously, white Western curricular, educational, economic, and political hegemony does not translate into "racial preference." White Western hegemony is "fair!"

With the U.C. Regents' ruling against affirmative action, I became my own kind of maniac, obsessively trying to fact-check, trying to better understand, this suddenly pivotal, this publicly welcomed "wedge" issue.

Gradually, I acquired a perspective consistent with what I learned.

AFFIRMATIVE ACTION emerged as a belated national policy some thirty years ago. Given a social predicament that plainly derived from American slavery and American hatred of men and women of African descent, President Lyndon Baines Johnson resolved in 1965 to "create equality in fact" for a people that "has been hobbled by chains." When President Johnson announced this affirmative resolve, his ambitions seemed minimal, and righteous, to everyone convinced that equality is an undebatable humane value appropriate to a democratic state.

Back then, a white majority population in the United States appeared to be assured. Back then, an economy either pursuing new modes of production, capital accumulation and profit, or else an economy expanding upon proven routes to the development of wealth appeared to be infinitely open.

In this context, affirmative action would not and did not seem necessarily threatening to the average white American: As long as you're eating well, you do not mind sharing your food with strangers.

Thirty years later, and we live in a country eager to imprison, detain, deport, defund anyone who is neither "white" nor native English-speaking.

Nevertheless, the white population of America is generally in decline while peoples of Spanish-speaking origins and Asian origins double or triple or quadruple their numbers. Any reliable population forecast for California and for the entire United States arrives at the same conclusion: a nonwhite majority within the lifespan of our children.

Simultaneous to this changing face of our electorate is our changing, our unrecognizable, our apparently running-away, economy. Internationalized and monopolized, our economy has become a game without rules. As would-be productive people, we rise and fall according to the outcome of these twin objectives underlying corporate management: the elimination of labor and the enlargement of profit.

Emerging demographic and economic structures herald the end of white American majority privilege and, also, the end of employment security for all levels of our national labor force.

These are the reasons for our pervasive uncertainty and flux.

These are the dynamics inducing uncontrollable, frightening change today.

Blackfolks are not responsible.

Women are not responsible.

Gay and lesbian and bisexual Americans are not responsible.

Undocumented immigrants are not responsible.

None of us is responsible for the awesome difficulties of this moment, but we have become the new American majority that will or will not survive these uncertainties and the divisive, scapegoating manipulations of the hateful among us.

Meanwhile and actually:

Affirmative action is what's left of our bloodstained aspirations toward universal civil rights. Affirmative action offers a moral alternative to national fratricide.

• • •

AT U.C.-BERKELEY, the most heterogeneous student population in the world attends a public institution of learning that, according to the "1995 National Research Council Report of Quality of Ph.D. Education in the United States," ranks number one. With thirty-five of our thirty-six Berkeley programs placing in the top ten, as the *New York Times* of September 13, 1995, exclaimed, "No other university even comes close!"

An earlier *Times* article from June 4, 1995, documents the following about U.C.–Berkeley during its ten-year adherence to affirmative action: In 1984, entering freshmen, mostly white (61 percent), presented an average SAT score of 1155 and a mean grade point average (GPA) of 3.62.

In 1994, entering freshmen (14 percent Hispanic, 6 percent Black, 32 percent white, and 39 percent Asian) presented an average SAT score of 1225 and a higher GPA of 3.84.

And an enormously important clarification about "Special Admissions" appeared in a sidebar to that *Times* report: For the school year 1994–95, only 3 percent of the entering freshmen came in through "Special Admissions" policy considerations such as economic disadvantages, rural background, musical abilities, physical disabilities, and race. As the director of admissions at U.C.–Berkeley, Bob Laird, explained to me, for the school year 1994–95, adhering to affirmative action criteria, 97 percent of all entering freshmen came from the top eighth of their class.

On January 19, 1996, the U.C. Board of Regents reconsidered its July 1995 decision against affirmative action. They agreed to this extraordinary second deliberation because their July decree provoked unanimous public denunciation and disclaimers from the then-president of the U.C. system, all nine chancellors, all faculty senates, and all student governments. In contrast to this legitimate educational community, the U.C. Board of Regents is composed of gubernatorial appointees like Ward Connerly, whose professional background can be more than adequately summarized as real-estate development.

On January 19, 1996, the U.C. Board of Regents voted to support its own decision against affirmative action. And so, whether or not our national media experts once more identify affirmative action as the pivotal "wedge" issue nationwide, all the lives, all the values, all the intended justice bespoken by that attempt at more equal, more democratic representation in the curriculum, in the classroom, and at the workplace, all remain at risk.

I look at this craziness and I try to return to a simplicity of perspective again.

But I cannot make that return.

The obvious, straightforward case for affirmative action and multicultural studies confronts such reckless ongoing misinterpretation and attack that we who support it find ourselves having to multiply our battle positions in response. In that multiplication, our simplicity of purpose becomes obscure.

And, because we can never get off the battlefield, we may not always acknowledge the complexities we encounter in our reach for new information. And we may feel it is too soon to begin an examination of our own moral conduct. But regardless of the power any of us does or does not possess, we must subject ourselves to just such scrutiny.

Yes, there is the truth of white Western domination.

Yes, there is the truth of our entitlement to self-respecting education about our distinctive human being, whether we derive from a Czechoslovakian, a Filipino, or a Nigerian heritage.

But we need to morally assess *the content* of our studies of our many selves, even as we affirm our disparate identities. Our studies will have to evolve into revolutionary, interactive confrontation with whatever we may discover.

We will have to embrace what my friend Peter Sellars invokes as "history as creative process," or we will merely become more fluently backward, more perfectly stuck in what the past can tell us about the past, good and evil, alike.

MARCH 1998: UPDATE ON AFFIRMATIVE ACTION

Implementation of Proposition 209 produced decimating reductions of African-American, Latino-American, and Native American students, 1997, entering University of California law schools, and schools of medicine.

Projected figures for freshman undergraduates entering U.C.–Berkeley in 1998 show a 50 to 70 percent drop in African-American and Latino-American students.

While graduate school administrations, and chancellors, sought new means to restore representative diversity on campus, statewide, the citizens of Houston, Texas, voted in November 1997, to preserve affirmative action: This solid majority vote reflects the pivotal importance of language. In contrast to Proposition 209, Houston's referendum plainly asked people to vote *for* or *against* affirmative action. The poisoning noun, *"preference,"* did not appear, anywhere.

As of March 1998, students at U.C.–Berkeley's Boalt Hall School of Law have launched an English Educational Opportunity Initiative that insists on plain English. If enough signatures can be secured, this initiative will reach the ballot box in November 2000.

GETTING DOWN
ON MY STREET

⋺⋲

1995

THIS IS ONE big country. And if people in North Dakota spoke one language, while folks in South Dakota or New Mexico, spoke another, a different, language, that would seem reasonable to me, even appropriate. And, so, I dispute all the various "nationwide" analyses and projections, each one colder than cold. "Nationwide" is too wide, too broad, to mean anything.

On the block where I live, there are Black families, white families, Southeast Asian–Americans, Chinese-Americans, "interracial" students, elderly folks, newlyweds, Jews, and Christians. This is a short little street of great good calm. And I defy anybody to identify more than two or three things that I may have in common with the household next door. They're Black. I'm Black. They live on this street. So do I. But what does race or residence in this city mean to them? I have no idea. And beyond that? Personally, I would not assume anything about them or anybody else on my block except that they're likely to be friendly in a California ("If you *ever* need anything . . .") way.

So when I started to read and hear about "the great racial divide," a week ago, I thought, "Sure. Is that something like Continental Drift? Or what?" And when I started to read and hear about race as the only and the biggest deal on the table, I thought, "Sure. Is that something like regular Black man Rodney King and multimillionaire O. J. Simpson equally symbolize what, exactly? And the fact that, for example, I'm female, is suddenly and forever beside the point?"

And, so, when some newspaper guy called from L.A. for a comment about the Million Man March, I said, "First of all, I was not invited. Second, I have one thing to say to and about anything or anybody who wants to sunder me from the Black man who is my son: 'You can go to hell!' "

And when a colleague (of sorts) of mine went off about domestic violence "versus" Mark Fuhrman and the LAPD, I said, "How come you can't see that Mark Fuhrman and the LAPD and racism, per se, suck Mack trucks, absolutely, yes, and, also, anybody who busts up his wife is totally reprehensible, and I don't forgive or forget anything or anybody who's just plain ugly and wrong: Mark Fuhrman *and* O. J. Simpson."

And when Minister Farrakhan proclaimed himself "God's Messenger" with not so much as a momentary twinkle of quasi-uneasiness, and when Minister Farrakhan went lyrical about the number nine symbolizing a pregnant woman with "a male child" inside her, and so on and so forth, I thought, "Well, there it is: CNN gives this guy two and a half hours of uninterrupted international television time—way more than the Pope, President Clinton, or Nelson Mandela—and then what?" More "nationwide" pseudoanalysis and projection about "the significance" of the importance that CNN, and most of the American mass media, invest Farrakhan with.

And then I read and I heard about who supported and who opposed the Million Man March, for a couple of days, but then, happily, happily, I realized that my local, real life preempts all of these national constructions and destructions.

• • •

ON THURSDAY, October 12, 1995, five thousand Americans of every description rallied at U.C.–Berkeley. There were "Queers for Affirmative Action," "Jews for Affirmative Action," "Asians for Affirmative Action," and Native American dances for affirmative action. Everybody was invited to the rally, and everybody showed up. As a matter of fact, the leadership for this fantastic success was a new U.C.–Berkeley student organization called Diversity in Action. As the name suggests, the members of this incredibly effective task force include African-American young men with dreads or shaved heads and Irish-American young men with blond ponytails and Chicana young women and Vietnamese-American young men and women, and like that, on and on.

This ecstatic, mighty throng gathered together to demand restoration of affirmative action throughout the University of California system, and to assert our intelligent resistance to demagogic, racialized, un-American manipulations that would deny American history, deplore American diversity, and destroy our manifest, principled unity.

When I spoke, I pointed to the very recent (September 12) finding by the 1995 National Research Council report on the quality of Ph.D. education in the United States: With the most heterogeneous student population in the world, U.C.–Berkeley is the leading, *the top*, university in America, or, as the *New York Times* reported, "No other university even comes close."

Our main speaker for this great day was the Reverend Jesse Jackson, and we greeted him with an endless tumult of genuine cheers and excitement. He came through with a rousing argument in favor of "real world" politics and policies and, therefore, affirmative action. He implored us to "turn to" each other and "not turn on" each other. He inveighed against the list of odious visions out here: racism, sexism, anti-Semitism, homophobia. And he implored us to get angry and vote Gingrich and company out of power in 1996.

On Tuesday, October 17, 1995, our U.C. faculty senate voted 124 to 2 to rescind the U.C. Regents' ruling against affirmative action. This vote does not mean the Regents will have to reverse themselves, but it does mean that the faculty stands with the students who stand with the chancellors, united in opposition to the Regents, and united in passionate support of affirmative action.

The "nationwide" assault on affirmative action began right here, in Northern California. And it looks to me like we may bury that particular outrage right here, where it was born. For sure, the fight is on, and it does seem far from hopeless.

So, yes, this is one big country. I happen to live on the Pacific Rim, which, for better or for worse, harbors the demographic and economic forecast for all of the USA in the twenty-first century.

And I trust what I can see and what I can hear and what I can do on my block, and around the corner, and on the campus where I teach.

And, just now, I am awfully glad to live nowhere else but here: right here.

ON TIME TANKA*

I refuse to choose
between lynch rope and gang rape
the blues is the blues!
My skin and my sex: Deep dues
I have no wish to escape

I refuse to lose
the flame of my single space
this safety I choose
between your fist and my face
between my gender and race

All Black and blue news
withers the heart of my hand
and leads to abuse

---

* A tanka is an ancient Japanese poetry form, consisting of a five-syllable line followed by a seven-syllable line, followed by a five-syllable line, followed by two seven-syllable lines.

no one needs to understand:
suicide wipes out the clues

Big-Time-Juicy-Fruit!
Celebrity-Rich-Hero
Rollin out the Rolls!
Proud cheatin on your (Black) wife
Loud beatin on your (white) wife

Real slime open mouth
police officer-true-creep
evil-and-uncouth
fixin to burn Black people
killin the song of our sleep

Neither one of you
gets any play in my day
I know what you do
your money your guns your say
so against my pepper spray

Okay! laugh away!
I hear you and I accuse
you both: I refuse
to choose: All Black and blue news
means that I hurt and I lose.

October 25, 1995

ON BISEXUALITY AND

CULTURAL PLURALISM

>€

Adapted from a Lecture at U.C.–Santa Cruz December 3, 1995.

PLURALISM HARDLY EVER comes up, in conversation. Once in a great while I'll hear that somebody "won" something by a "plurality" of votes, and that always sounds weird. Right away I'm wondering, does that mean s/he got more votes, or what? It's not clear. It's not *win* or *lose*. It's not *yes* or *no*.

Because I live inside the same popular culture that saturates the consciousness of my neighbors, I am conditioned to regard "clarity" as the construction of reality in terms of either/or. For example: You love me or you do not. You love me or you love somebody else. These formulations presumably lead to clear conclusions that void, or avoid, complexities such as, "You love me and I am not the only woman you love." But complexity is the essence of everything real.

And so I find myself increasingly resistant to allegedly "simple" anything. I don't trust "simple." I don't believe in it. And, with our Western bent toward insidious evaluation, and analysis, I worry about the dangerous, Aristotelian, here-or-not-here implications of "simple."

So I turn to the concept of *pluralism*. Is that a start, at least, toward an intellectual illumination of our complex identities and experience?

According to the American Heritage Dictionary of the English Language, Third Edition, "pluralism" is "the condition of being plural"; "a condition of society in which numerous distinct ethnic, religious, or cultural groups coexist within one nation"; "the doctrine that reality is composed of many ultimate substances"; "the belief that no simple explanatory system or view of reality can account for all the phenomena of life."

And, after thinking about these definitions, I arrive at my own related ideas:

A. *A democratic philosophy of cultural pluralism:* A society in which numerous distinct ethnic and racial and religious groups *rightfully* and *equally* CO-exist within one nation.
B. *Sexual pluralism:* A condition in which one person advocates and/or adheres to two or more kinds of sexuality.
C. *A democratic philosophy of sexual pluralism:* That advocating and/or adhering to more than one kind of sexuality is duly consistent with individual and collective values basic to the creation, and the upkeep of cultural pluralism *per se* (of, the value of *freedom*).

IN MY POCKET I have twenty-six cents: one quarter and one penny, official American currency decorated by the Latin inscription *E Pluribus Unum*. For a long time I thought nothing in particular about that particular motto, "from many, one." It seemed to make (common) sense if only because I'd never heard any ideas to the contrary.

But actually that's a pretty dangerous notion: *E Pluribus Unum*.

Unless we're looking at strawberries and bananas and kiwi California smoothies, "from many, one" could mean some awful, even horrifying state policies and beliefs. It could mean the Aryan race. It could mean ethnic cleansing. It could mean apartheid. It could mean the Naturalization Act of 1790, which decreed that only white people could become naturalized citizens of the United States.

It could mean "English only" legislation. It could mean I'd better forget about who I really am, or why; it could mean I'd better identify with that dominant force, I'd better embrace and espouse that domination.

But also, *E Pluribus Unum* is not God's truth, or God's plan. How we got here, as a species, for example, does not support that ambition, *E Pluribus Unum*. And, in general, evolution flows in an opposite direction. Evolution flows into diversity by dint of infinite diversification: *from The One, many.*

If you put something on your money I would assume you mean it and the fact that *E Pluribus Unum* appears on my twenty-six cents suggests that, as a cultural and sexual pluralist, I am in serious trouble here. I am swimming in too many rivers
because

A. There should only be one river.

and

B. That one river should be speeding on its way from *one* starting point to *one* destination.

Get with it!

What is my problem?

How can I fail to accept the simple truth/the natural state of affairs/ the divine order of whatever prevails, whatever dominates?

Especially when whatever prevails, whatever dominates, protects its power through cautionary folk tales, primitive law, and state-initiated or state-sanctioned violence, then how can I deny those simple truths so abundantly wedged inside popular consciousness? For instance, Western civilization:

Why would I want to disturb that unified, that deified, focus with some sort of multicultural rearrangement?

And, anyway, *multicultural?* Doesn't that imply a harebrained hodgepodge leading to explorations of no intellectual validity? Multicultural! Doesn't that imply something unlimited, which is to say chaotic and nonlinear and nonhierarchical and open-ended and, therefore, possessing no intellectual validity?

Why do I want to know French and Chinese? Why do I think I need to travel to Calcutta, Osaka, Luande, Dar es Salaam, Belfast, and Brooklyn, along with London, Amsterdam, or Rome?

Why don't I settle down in central Idaho, study the rise and fall of the Prussian Empire, and watch a little football on the telly?

What's the matter with me?

Or why should I be curious about my complicated heritage:

My mother, Afro-Caribbean and East Indian
My father, Euro-Caribbean and Chinese
My childhood: East Coast-Urban-Negro-Community and
    Universe
My education: virtually all-Black public school followed by
    virtually all-white prep school and Ivy
League college.
Why should I be concerned? Should I fathom these varying
    parts and then attempt to
configurate them into a coherent, but nonhierarchical whole
    of many varying parts?
I should choose one!
My father or my mother/my neighborhood or my prep
    school.
I should simplify and stabilize!
From many, one!

And, besides, how do I dare dismiss common arguments against cultural pluralism:

1. That it consigns Western civilization to a lottery that may not defer to white or Western supremacy;
2. That it complicates that picture so that distinctions blur from among different peoples of color, for example. Accordingly,

some marginalized groups fear they _____ -
ginal visibility.

I am a cultural pluralist because I am i_____ t
else should I be? Given that I see and I hea_____ d
me in this one country of ours, what else sh___

I am in my right mind.

And, therefore, I do not propose that tho_____ d
be homogenized into one prime-time sitco_____ s
Unum as a guideline or goal. I have to!

Yes, I understand the hierarchical urge of individuals and groups wanting to imitate or, better yet, merge with Dominant Culture because, otherwise, they fear disastrous dependency, invisibility, or extinction. And I even understand the pathological urge to act like the Number Ones; I understand the urge to copycat the hateful, violent, and disgusting, dominant history of dominant response to those who differ from those who would dominate.

But that hierarchical urge is antidemocratic, at least, and, I believe, immoral, besides. That hierarchical urge to be The One out of the many (or despite the many), that urge to be The One above The Others cannot be satisfied for any individual or any groups of individuals except at the expense—except at the possibly exterminating expense—of another individual or group.

And so, I am a cultural pluralist: from the one, many, many, many. Because many is natural. Because many is always happening—more and more, in fact. And many is the way things will continue to proliferate and abound—short of some 1990s Final Solution to the many perceived as A Problem.

Yes I am in favor of the absolute unqualified preservation of the complicated, pluralist society that already exists, whether we like it or not! I favor this completely, this pluralism, because I am not a supremacist of any sort, whatsoever. And I persist inside a critical experiment which must confer equal rights and equal protection upon the many, one by one, or fail as a democracy.

Now, any examination of culture must include the psychology as well as the biology of its specifics: the mind of the body and the body of the mind. Nowhere is this indivisibly dual dynamic more obvious than inside the sphere of human sexuality.

Sexuality, like culture writ large, has been subjected to the *E Pluribus Unum* approach to diversity for a long time. Regardless of the physical and emotional varieties of sexual interest/desire/need represented by the variety of human beings that we, all of us, make manifest, the *E Pluribus Unum* Club of Dominant Culture—members only—would have us accept that sexuality is something clear/something simple/basic/God-given, or, in short, heterosexual.

I would agree with *basic* and with *God-given* if, by God-given, you mean extant, here; in existence, for real.

But simple? Gosh, I don't think so!

Somehow I have never noticed a remarkable simplicity peculiar to or employed by heterosexual men and women! And yet, a hefty part of the *E Pluribus Unum* sexuality campaign rests upon claims like "diamonds are forever" and heterosexuality is "simple" because it's "dominant," because it's "simple," and so forth—"forever."

On the other hand, I have noticed a remarkable Dominant Culture inclination to define sexuality in its own heterosexual image—and to exclude/criminalize/derogate/vilify any other sexuality.

I am a cultural pluralist. And, as sexuality is a biological, psychological, and interpersonal factor of cultural experience, I am a sexual pluralist.

What else could I be?

Given men who desire women and women who desire men and men who desire men and women who desire women and men who want to become women and women who want to become men and men who desire men and women both, and women who desire women and men both, what else could I be, besides a sexual **pluralist?**

I understand why women who identify themselves as lesbians and why men who identify themselves as gay might wish to ostracize, or condemn, bisexuality. It is that fearful emulation of the history of the Dominant Culture's response to those who differ/who choose to be different. It is fear that an already marginalized and jeopardized status will become confused and or obscured and/or extinguished by yet another complicated sexual reality seeking its safety and its equal rights.

But you cannot draw the line on freedom, you cannot draw the line on equality. And if I am not free and if I am not equally entitled to love and desire both men and women, in other words,

> if I am not free and if I am not entitled equal to heterosexuals
>   and homosexuals
> then
> homosexual men and women have joined with the dominant
>   heterosexual culture in the tyrannical
> pursuit of *E Pluribus Unum*
> and I
> a bisexual woman committed to cultural pluralism and,
>   therefore to sexual pluralism, can only
> say, you better watch your back!

Any abridgment of anybody's right to exist places in jeopardy each one of us, regardless of race, class, religion, ethnicity, sexuality, gender, proportional size.

So I am a cultural pluralist. I am a sexual pluralist. And to those who do not agree with me I say, "Good luck!"

EYEWITNESS IN

LEBANON

⊰⊱

1996

WHEN AMERICAN PUNDITS talk about "The Middle East," they mean Israel: what favors or what threatens Israeli interests.

And so, for example, the country and the people of Lebanon no longer exist because Israeli leaders have decided to focus upon Syria, Jordan, and Turkey "to the North."

Hence, when you come upon a listing of Middle Eastern states in our own media, you rarely will find Lebanon anywhere on the page.

If I had not recently traveled to Lebanon, I would probably note this currently commonplace omission as "disquieting" or "odd."

But I went there, to Lebanon. And I'm back. And I'm real. And Lebanon is real. And this poisonous pretense to the contrary seems to me insolent and ominous, at best.

What's the brainstorm here: that if Israel and the United States agree to "disappear" Lebanon, then whenever Israel follows up its various invasions of that tiny place with outright annexation, nobody will notice because Lebanon will have become nowhere, anyway?

This is my eyewitness reaction to the country and the people of Lebanon. This is my eyewitness reaction to the Israeli sixteen-day war against Lebanon. It is not welltempered.

My life requires perpetual revolt against a double standard that puts me on the Easily Invisible side of the ledger, the Don't Matter and No Count side of things, the Be Good/Keep Quiet/Say "Thank You" side of the equation.

And Lebanon is on the wrong side, just like me. Lebanon is not white. Lebanon is not overwhelmingly Christian or Jewish or European. It's an Arab nation.

It's very small. It's half the size of Israel, which is the size of Massachusetts. And even including what's left of the 300,000-plus refugees who sought shelter there after their expulsion from Palestine in 1948, the total population of Lebanon is half that of Israel.

When Israel forced more than 400,000 Lebanese citizens to flee from their homes and villages, that amounted to 14 percent of the entire population.

A truly huge number of women and children were suddenly rendered homeless.

Lebanon maintains the only democratic Arab government. Arab peoples regard Lebanon as the heart of Arab culture, and for a long time almost every political and artistic movement in the world found its way into the cafés and secret meeting places of Beirut.

Today there is scarcely a structure in all of Beirut that does not bear the markings of shrapnel. The downtown area resembles the ruins of Pompeii. Everywhere you see soldiers and gigantic construction cranes revising the scenery before your eyes.

I went to Lebanon because I believe that Arab peoples and Arab-Americans occupy the lowest, the most reviled spot in the racist mind of America.

I went because I believe that to be Muslim and to be Arab is to be a people subject to the most uninhibited, lethal bullying possible.

Why isn't it general knowledge that the United States success-fully introduced U.N. Resolution 425 in 1978, calling for the imme-diate and unconditional Israeli withdrawal from Lebanon? That reso-lution has never been revoked—or enforced.

Why isn't it general knowledge that Israel "occupies" southern Lebanon in absolute violation of international law, U.N. Resolution 425, and the sovereign rights of the people of Lebanon?

How does it happen that Hezbollah becomes synonymous with "terrorist" when members and followers of Hezbollah are, actually, Lebanese men who live in Lebanon and who have won substantial representation in the Lebanese parliament and who are fighting the illegal Israeli occupation of Lebanese land?

What will it take before "terrorist" becomes the adjective at-tached to Israeli depredations that include massacres of civilians and the calculated destruction of water reservoirs and electrical power plants?

When will we establish and abide by a No Exceptions policy: the same one standard for valuation of human life and the moral mea-surement of our deeds?

On Monday, May 6, 1996, the top headline of England's *The Independent* declared: MASSACRE FILM PUTS ISRAEL IN DOCK. In an exclusive report by Robert Fisk, the facts of Israeli knowledge of the massacre at the U.N. refugee camp at Qana appeared, accompanied by still photos from a video film of the entire assault. The Israelis murdered two hundred women and children. These were refugees taking shelter inside the U.N. compound, and the Israelis knew their exact location.

When the story came out, I thought: Here was the Rodney King video of the Middle East. At last, here was incontrovertible evidence of Israeli lies and Israeli savagery that no one could now refute.

Surely even Bill Clinton would be forced to become less uncon-ditional in his support of Israel. Perhaps even the multibillion-dollar habit of aid to Israel would finally be reexamined and curtailed.

But my relief was naive. That video is the Rodney King video of the Middle East, but Arab life is less than and lower than African-

American life, and so nothing happened. This incontrovertible evidence of Israel's planned massacre received nominal notice on the news and then, like Lebanon, it disappeared.

What did I see in Lebanon? I saw a poor, dusty stretch of difficult earth between the sea and the mountains.

I saw the darkness and I felt the chill and I beheld the squalor of what we like to call "refugee camps."

I saw a six-year-old girl with no family left, and a parking lot full of orphan boys and girls.

I saw a man bereft of his wife and nine children.

I saw the mangled materials of a house bombed into nothing usable.

I saw death and I heard death and death is not beautiful, and sometimes the lamentations for the dead clouded the air.

I heard Prime Minister Rafik Hariri saying, "We have the feeling of proud" because not everyone had died.

I savored sweet coffee reasons for solidarity with Lebanese resistance to anti-Arab and anti-Muslim hatred and assault.

I saw overwhelming variations on grief beyond all language.

I watched a woman setting out a jasmine plant that would probably manage the atmosphere and, possibly, flourish.

Notes Toward a Model
of Resistance

⋙⋘

Keynote for the 1996 San Francisco Conference of The National Coalition

Against Sexual Assault.

1996

RAPE IS NOT something I think about. I mean, not ordinarily.

Feelings surround and submerge that dread, familiar possibility. And they radiate as clear and as predictable as a relentless shredding of flesh.

But to move from a mostly reactive mode into analysis, I have made myself examine that violence as a classical interplay between the powerful and the powerless.

There is, of course, a "classical" outcome to that nonequation, namely, domination on the winning side and surrender on the other.

So I had been hoping to arrive at a rational means to a new conclusion, a different victory. But I couldn't get anywhere, just forcing the issue into my consciousness.

And, then, all this past week, my students and I became consumed by our need to invent an affirmative action on behalf of affirmative action.

Having lost California's electoral fight by 54 to 46 percent in our fight to retain affirmative action in public education and the workplace, we asked ourselves what could we, the losers, do?

Faced with the power of an opponent majority, what could we, the powerless, do now?

We decided to fast, and to demonstrate, and to organize, and to publicize—as an indivisible, publicly manifest collective.

Fasting let us test ourselves: What was the strength, what was the depth, of our resolve?

Collective identity, deliberations, and political display served to tighten our cohesion as an effective group, and to reinforce our individual struggle against compromise, or failure.

Organizing meant outreach beyond ourselves and return benefits from a supportive, and widening, network of allies.

Publicizing our effort absolutely confirmed our intention to resist defeat.

Demonstrating publicly in a militant vigil maintained through rain or sunshine reified our rhetoric and verified through deeds the promise of our words.

Choosing a Specific Target for Counterattack, in this instance, San Francisco's CNN studios, brought "the enemy" into manageable scale and weakened the abstract force of our abstract 56 percent opponent.

Coalescing, however possible, reassured us of our growing power and, in addition, opened our undertaking to creative input beyond our best, but necessarily limited, brainstorm.

Underlying all of the above was our repeated, and deliberate, confrontation with fear: fear of the enemy and fear of our own *apparent* impotence.

And, throughout, we licensed ourselves to acknowledge and work with our undeniable rage.

So it began to occur to me that perhaps we were building our model for resistance to domination, one model for resistance to power opposed to your rights and your needs for safe and self-respecting self-determination.

Last Thursday, things came to a climax. We had decided not to seek a permit for our demonstration because we fully intended to continue to conduct ourselves as a peaceful assembly of citizens and because we knew that the right to such assembly is guaranteed by the U.S. Constitution.

Once we reached the sidewalk outside those CNN studios, the chief security guard launched into a nonstop harassment routine: He was going to call the police. We were going to be arrested. We were trespassing. We were disturbing passersby and blocking their access to ATM machines, and so forth.

I urged him to go ahead and make that call. And very soon there were three police cars with their flashing lights and a really excited, loud security guard yelling lies and various accusations.

Suddenly, this was armed force on the scene. And the question was how would that power be deployed.

I spoke with one police officer after another, searching for somebody who happened to know about the U.S. Constitution.

Things got pretty tense.

And it was a good five minutes before, purely by chance, I found myself laughing with one cop who, yes, had heard of the Constitution and who also happened to have heard about the constitutional right to peaceful assembly.

Thanks to that piece of luck, the police withdrew, and our vigil proceeded as we'd planned.

Meanwhile, I was making mental notes about what had seemed to work in the context of a showdown.

I came up with this list: absence of fear; affirmation of self-worth; resolute holding to one's entitlement to the power one was exercising; manifest support; calls to other, not manifest support, such as sympathetic media, legal counsel, and kindred student organizations; and the stunning energy of rage.

Inside this volatile mix, a woman who had volunteered to help us, as needed, fell apart. She was, she is, an attorney. And when the scene got crowded and chancy, we'd asked her to vouch for the U.S. Constitution and its pertinence to our case. We'd asked her to tell the police that there is a United States Constitution and that that document guarantees citizens the right to peaceful assembly. That's all. But when she saw the cop cars and their flashing lights, and when she heard the loud anger of the accusatory security guard, she lost it.

Rather than speak to the police, she started to tremble and cry. She said to me, "I can't. I can't do this. I'm just a single mother with three children." And so on.

And it was awful to watch her fear making her powerless. It was awful. It was very depressing.

And I thanked her for showing up, anyway.

And I watched her retreat: Not blessed by a visible, known, tested, and building community on which she could rely, she felt, and, therefore, she was isolated. She could not do herself, or anyone else, any good.

I think this has something to do with rape, which, I think, has a lot to do with domination and the dominator's determination to deprive you of your rights.

And after our weeklong vigil for affirmative action, I have come to believe that some patterns of resistance offer a better chance for victory than others.

Both times I was raped I was

by myself.
I was isolated.
I did not possess a manifest
or an invisible-but-known-and-building
community.

Both times I was shocked by what was happening as it was happening and, therefore,

I lost force lost speed
needed

for resistance.
And I think that the costly paralysis
of my shock
directly devolved from my
isolation,
from my not knowing other women
who had been raped,
from my not knowing that rape
happens mostly between men
that you take for granted as
a friendly part of your
regular life
and yourself, your body
suddenly
chosen for violent domination: Chosen for rape.

The first time the man who raped me was white. And he was, I
thought, a friend, of sorts. Not close, but part of my friendly and
taken-for-granted, regular environment.
        The shock of that episode
capsized me into nausea and
a sense of self-loathing and
a conviction of absolute powerlessness
until he got to a point
where he was trying
to wrestle me into the shower
and he had turned
the water on
and the soap fell
to the ground and he yelled,
"Pick it up."
He was ordering me to pick it up!
And that snapped me out
of the paralysis of self-loathing
because I thought two things:
I thought

(a) This is a white man trying to make me do something
and (b) This is a monster
who wants me to bend over
and pick up a piece of soap
so he can sodomize me
here and now on top of
everything he has done
to me for the past
45 minutes. And
I said to that man
I said,
"You pick it up!"
And I couldn't believe I had found my voice again
but I had,
and that was what I said to him.
And he was just a bit more surprised
than I was that I had found my
voice.
And I was from that moment
resolute;
I was from that moment
fearless:
The only thing left for him to do to me
was kill me,
And I did not care any more about that;
I just knew this was it: This was my limit!
I would not bend over and pick
up that piece of soap for that white man.

And we stared at each other
And then he tried to laugh and
regain "mastery" over the "situation"
and so, still
laughing, he bent down to
pick up the soap

and as he did that
I knocked him forward
onto his head.
And I fled from the
shower the bathroom
I fled from my own house
naked
and terrified and freezing
but free.
And I was looking then for
a community I could not find anywhere
at that hour of the night in that American small town of East
Hampton.

Well, the aftermath was lengthy and convoluted
and dense with self-loathing still.
And, eventually, it did occur to me that,
until race entered the dynamics
of that episode,
I had been unable to find within myself
the righteous certainty
that resistance
requires
the righteous certainty that would explode my paralysis
and bring me to an "over my dead
body"
determination
to stop
his violence
stop
his violation of everything that I am.

I mean
it took me a while to notice that finally
I could get to a "do or die" level
of rage

only by focusing upon the fact that
he was a white man
ordering me
a Black woman
around.
I could not reach my self-protective
rage on any other basis: for example, on the basis of the fact
that A Man was raping me, A Woman,
or that in other words
somebody way stronger than I am was forcing himself
upon me—somebody unable to defend
herself against his hatred his contempt for me, for women.
And I thought so then,
and I think now, that there is a huge, known
community out here working against racism
and racist violence.
But violence against women
did not have
and does not have a remotely comparable
huge and known community
working against that pathology that
saturates
popular consciousness,
that pathology that depicts
women and girls as troublesome
idiots or unbearable bitches or
uncontrollable whores or
the Eve Root of all
Evil;
that pathology of perspective
upon everyone female
that makes it possible
for the majority cultures of the world
to abort girl babies,
   or drown them,
   or suffocate them,

or leave them to starve on the streets,
or tie them to a tiny chair until
they / these girl babies
cry themselves to death;
that saturating pathology of perspective imposed upon
  everyone female
makes rape
an inevitability,
not an exceptional situation of horror but an inevitability!

The second time I was raped the man was Black—
He was, in fact, head of the local NAACP.
And I'd met him at a bar when a community
(I thought) of my friends from a writers'
colony went out, a whole bunch of us, one
night, to celebrate my birthday.
He had introduced himself to us and to me. And we'd
danced. And, as the bar was closing, around 2 A.M.,
he'd invited all of us to his house for
bacon and eggs and coffee.
So we all, I thought, headed over there.
Except, when I arrived, I discovered
my community had disappeared.
Nobody else showed up.
I waited around, chatting, nervously, for five
or ten minutes.
When it seemed clear no one else
was coming
I said good night and started toward
the door,
and that's when this friendly, head of the
local NAACP Black man
raped me.

Again, I was shocked and so I lost force
and speed of resistance.
How could this be happening?

He was Black.
I was Black.
Et cetera. Et cetera.

When I got out of that house I stood still.
It was dawn.
My body ached all over.
I thought I must be the most defiled,
the filthiest thing in the world.
I could not bear the idea of seeing or speaking
with anyone.
I drove back to my studio.
I went into the bathroom and I put soap
all over my tongue
and I threw up
and I soaped my tongue again
and I washed
and I scrubbed
and I vomited
and I cried
and all the while I was thinking,
I was asking, How could he do this to me?

I was wasting my energies on this
rapist this pig monster
who
left me feeling so low-down
it was
more than a year before I could
tolerate any man or even any
male student of mine anywhere
closer than ten feet away from me.

I freaked out
from that experience of brute domination.
I lived terrified, completely

I refused even to contemplate
sex with anybody.
I denied the possible help of therapy.
I wanted nobody to touch me ever again.
I isolated myself.
I lived inside my fear.
I rejected even the concept
of a community to which I might
belong or a community that might
belong to me.

Much has happened since then.
I have been loved by men and women
wiser and more tenderly patient
than I can describe.
And so I have overcome much of
that self-loathing and that terror
—but not all of it.
I don't think you can ever completely
"recover" from rape. I'm not sure
what that would mean, really, unless
you denied some crucial part of that violent
debasement that actually took place
upon you and against your actual person.

But, again, in the instance of that second rape, the issue of race was
pivotal, except, this time, race paralyzed me to the deadly extent of
self-effacement.

Shocked that a "Brother" would violate me his "Sister,"
I lost speed and resolute force of resistance
and I never I never tapped into the rage
necessary for resistance
to the demons of domination.

And, so, subsequently, it became clear to me that I had a whole
lot of profound and overdue thinking to begin on the subject of
what it means to be female regardless of color.

In this world it is very dangerous,
everywhere, to be female.
For one thing,
it means you will never have the kind of
money and stupid celebrity or upper-class clout of
an O. J. Simpson or a
Ted Kennedy or a Mike Tyson
or a William Kennedy Smith or an Alex Kelly.
For another, it means that a universal double
standard will plague your every effort
to live free and equal.

For example, in Catholic countries of Central and South America it is not unusual for a husband to murder his wife because he believes she's been unfaithful to him, and then that husband is *not* sent to prison. Likewise, it is not unusual for a man to murder his (former) girlfriend with impunity, if it's a "crime of passion."

In Islamic culture, adhering to the Qur'an means that a woman accused of adultery can be stoned to death and/or should be jailed and left to die without food or water while no such punishments are prescribed for men accused of and/or guilty of adultery, and so forth.

And in this polyglot America it is commonplace mores that
    mean
it's okay that O. J. Simpson was never
faithful to either of his two wives and
that he was totally sexually active after he and Nicole
    divorced,
but it is incriminating of Nicole Simpson
that she,
after divorcing O.J., had sexual relations
with other men.
It is, as I said, a universal double standard
that assaults the very baseline notion
of equality for female human beings.

It means that you have Army Commanders, with a straight face, declaring that they "can't believe" Tailhook and now Aberdeen documentations of male abuse of male power over and above and against female members of the Armed Forces. And then you have male owned and male staffed media reporting such outrageous lies as "news" to the rest of us.

How could anybody claim to be incredulous about documented rape of women in the armed forces of the United States?

According to the *New York Times* of November 17, 1996, less than ten years ago, Marine Corps drill instructors still led training runs with chants like: "One, two, three, four. Everyday we pray for war. Five, six, seven, eight. Rape. Kill. Mutilate."

Moreover, the *New York Times* describes this milieu as "a warrior culture." Not a diseased culture or not a monstrous perversion of culture but "a warrior culture" (and any child can tell you that A Warrior is, by definition: a hero!).

But still much, if not nearly, not nearly enough, has changed over the past twenty years.

And this is why there is this conference this week celebrating twenty-five years of "rape crisis centers" and the attempted public and legal construction of a community of increasing safety and of power for women.

And I am very very happy and cheered to acknowledge these past twenty-five years as an irreversible awakening of resistance consciousness and spirit, even though it often seems that the more you find out the more you realize you need to find out—and change. It is also indisputable that first we have to fathom the complexity and the depth of our crisis before we can hope to rescue any single girl or woman from lifelong, universal threats to her safe assertion of her human rights, her self-determination, inside every moment and on every level.

I would like to reiterate what I have learned this week on the streets of San Francisco with my students about resistance to intentional, violent domination—which is the meaning of the passage of California's Proposition 209:

- Testing ourselves for strength of resolve/fasting
- Meeting as a collective
- Reaching out for support
- Asking media to spread the word: *Resistance*
- Public vigil
- Determining a specific target for counterattack
- Commitment to perseverance and coalition
- Confrontation of one's fears
    Fear of the enemy
    Fear of our own *apparent* impotence
- Tapping into necessary, righteous rage
- Inexhaustible work on all of the above.

By going beyond rhetoric, and by putting our heads and our bodies on the street, resolute, for the sake of affirmative action, I think we have found one valid model for resistance to rape.

BESTING A WORST CASE

SCENARIO

⋇

Keynote for the Mayor's Summit on Breast Cancer, San Francisco, California, November 1996.

ON A VERY pleasant afternoon, my best friend and I went to see the doctor.

He was also very pleasant, this local oncologist: affable, even, and just this side of avuncular; unctuous.

Highly recommended by my regular physician, I sat across from him, from Dr. Gardner, listening and alert.

He spoke without hesitation: "From my own examination, and from what the mammograms indicate, I'd say you could go ahead and wait to have a biopsy for five, or even ten years. There's absolutely no hurry, no need to worry!"

At this point, my friend exclaimed: "But what if the biopsy could turn out positive?"

Dr. Gardner smiled such a warm, big smile. "Don't even think about that! It's not a possibility!"

That was the 1992 beginning of my immersion in breast cancer medical care, breast cancer mythologies, breast cancer mistakes, breast cancer mysteries, breast-cancer-mastectomy-as-an-allegedly-conservative-medical-mentality, and shattering, numerously incidental mess-ups of an inexcusable, irreversible, untoward, and truly personal, nature.

Ready or not, as I soon learned, one gets stuck with the consequences of all this.

I was not ready.

I didn't know anything about breast cancer.

What caused it? Could it kill you? How many people had it? Does it feel a certain way or mean something particular about you or your past history or your future?

Meanwhile, something about Dr. Gardner bothered me. I didn't quite believe the comfortable posturing of his tone. If everything was so sunny and nice, why was his waiting room so eerie and dim?

Why had I been urged to consult with him "as soon as possible"?

And why did my gut tell me to schedule the biopsy as fast as I could make that happen?

I followed my gut.

And two weeks after the smiling assurances of Dr. Gardner, I remember coming out of general anesthesia, and there was my regular physician, my friend, Dr. Allen Steinbach, hovering close above my face, and calling my name:

"June!" he repeated. "June! Can you hear me? There's bad news!"

I thought, *Bad news? Had something god-awful happened to my son? My lover? One of my students?*

DR. STEINBACH gripped my shoulders and held me still:

"We found cancer. It's
cancer. You have
breast cancer."

I could tell from his voice that he was not joking / not just trying to get my attention. But, beyond that, I felt nothing.

I did not know what "breast cancer" means.
I had no idea.

But from the moment of that finding of cancer in my right breast, my days and nights capsized into a worst case scenario I am still battling to outwit.

And I am still at a loss about how I should wage that battle for my life.

Nobody knows.

And that totally pisses me off.

I mean, like, why not?

One in eight women in the USA will be diagnosed with invasive breast cancer: one in eight!

Every year there are 183,000 cases of breast cancer reported, in the USA, and

every year
every year
every single year
46,000 women die from breast cancer.

The mortality rate for breast cancer is higher, significantly higher, than the mortality rate for AIDS. And yet far more public awareness has been primed on behalf of AIDS—far more—than for this steady, pervasive killer: Breast Cancer.

How come?

According to San Francisco's Department of Health,

- 6 women die from breast cancer every hour
- 144 women die from breast cancer every day
- 1,008 women die from breast cancer every week
- 4,032 women die from breast cancer every month

And *"25 percent of all the women diagnosed with breast cancer in any given year will die within five years."*
And *"50 percent of all women diagnosed within any given year will die within ten years."*

This is a national disgrace.
This is a soft-spoken emergency.
This is a colossal loss of life
lost to a colossal absence of
uncontrollable, serious, coast-to-coast,
around-the-clock, no-nothing-as-usual,
outcry and civil
and uncivil disobedience
to a status quo that includes such
unbelievably huge numbers of women
suffering and dying
at a predictable rate
during predictable time periods

What's up?

In the last twenty years in the United States, 3,660,000 women have perished from the disease known as breast cancer.

Twenty years later, and nobody knows the cause of this disease?

Twenty years later, and maybe a low-fat diet will help to avoid or retard the spread of that disease, but maybe a low-fat diet has nothing to do with it?

Twenty years later, and maybe childbearing and maybe lengthy breastfeeding will help to avoid or retard the spread of that disease, but maybe not? Maybe childbearing and breastfeeding have nothing to do with breast cancer and who gets it and who does not?

Twenty years later and maybe regular exercise and maybe over-weight and maybe meditation or maybe visualizations or maybe group-sharing or maybe mastectomies or maybe chemotherapy or maybe Japanese pickled plums will cure or arrest or prevent breast cancer or maybe not?

In a downtown department store in Norfolk, Virginia, the sales-woman asks me if I'd like to pin a pretty pink ribbon onto my T-shirt.

"For what?" I ask her.

"Oh, just to show your awareness of breast cancer," she tells me pleasantly.

She seems like an okay person, not somebody obviously meant for a lunatic asylum and yet she's offering me a little strip of pretty pink ribbon to show my awareness of breast cancer, which, actually, is the reason I didn't wear T-shirts, unless they were way extra-large, for a full two years after I underwent a mastectomy, which, I was told, would increase my odds of survival and which, in fact, did not.

But I am getting ahead of my story. And I want to tell this story because I don't want it to become part of an ongoing, general her-story. I want my story to help to raise red flags, public temperatures, holy hell, public consciousness, blood pressure, and morale—activist/research/victim morale so that this soft-spoken emergency becomes the number-one-on-the-tip-of-the-tongue issue all kinds of people join to eradicate, this afternoon/tonight/Monday morning.

So when I received the written report of the biopsy performed on my right breast from the hospital I noticed that the malignancy had been attributed to my left breast.

And I thought that was a major, unpardonable mistake. And I still think so.

But there were others.

Prior to the mastectomy procedure, which my next oncologist urged me to agree to, I was told that if I had the procedure I would have an 80 percent chance of surviving more than five years. A mastectomy would secure those 80 percent odds in my favor.

You may appreciate, then, my disbelief, and dismay, when, after undergoing that surgery, my oncologist told me that I now had only a 40 percent prognosis for survival over the next five years. The odds had changed, absolutely, because the mastectomy procedure had discovered that the malignancy had spread into the lymph nodes and there was, now, no way to track, or even to try to locate, let alone eliminate, the dread interior dissemination of the disease.

But let me backtrack to a few weeks before I heard 40 percent as my new number/my worst case scenario.

The surgeon who performed the mastectomy came highly recommended and, indeed, one week after the operation, I saw him featured in a big article about all-star San Francisco medical care.

And he was extremely nice. And he was very pleasant. And he was very reassuring.

But he was going on vacation, actually, the morning after he performed a mastectomy on me.

In fact, I remember his coming by in his Top-Siders and leather jacket and plaid shirt and jeans, looking as cheerful as anybody could be about to get out and away, and I remember wishing him a swell vacation and I meant that, of course.

But then he forgot to tell whoever to make sure to check and to empty the drain he had installed in the wound site, and so shortly after he waved good-bye to me and disappeared, yet another crisis materialized.

Because no one was checking the drain and letting out the blood, the tissue of the wound site became perilously thin and un- able to generate new cells and the questions were

would I ever stop bleeding from that wound site
and also would skin or flesh of any kind ever develop there,
    anew, or not?
I will spare you the details of that crisis, but you should
    understand that those
details meant that various sorts of hideous dressings on the
    wound site had to
be changed daily and I could not bear to look at the dressings
    or the wound
site and who among my devoted friends could really tolerate
    those details,
which they (my devoted friends) did nevertheless tolerate and
    attempt to
ameliorate nevertheless
And those details meant that I had to move around with a
    drain still installed
in the wound site for a very long time after the surgery
and that meant that
for a very long time after the surgery,

I had to make myself measure the holdings of the drain and
   let out the blood
and so on
and those details meant that
even when,
after a very long time,
the drain was finally removed,
the question of bleeding persisted
and so
I was told to not use not move my
right arm for months,
and that means and
and that meant that
(I was and I am a right-handed
writer and poet
for instance
who writes by hand every word
that she writes)
I could write nothing
for months,
and it was not clear,
for months,
if I would again ever be able to use and to move my right
   arm/my right
hand/it was not clear for months if I would write again/
   because the
question of bleeding from
the wound site
and the question of cell regeneration
remained unanswered questions for a very long time.
And
if I may remind you,
all of this happened
on top of a mastectomy
because my surgeon forgot to tell somebody

to check and to empty the drain he
installed in my wound site.
It was a breast cancer mistake.
Of course, maybe my surgeon was distracted
not only by his imminent vacation but
also because there had been another mistake:
Subsequent to the mastectomy something
else had gone wrong and because I was
a patient in a teaching institution
apparently there was discussion and even
debate among several doctors and resident
interns as to What Should Happen Next
and the result was
that, some hours after the mastectomy,
I lay in critical condition
with a plummeted blood pressure reading
and a bunch of well-meaning upright guys
pursuing an argument
around my semi-comatose body.

Luckily, however, my best friend got a
5 alarm phone call from a concerned
registered nurse on the premises, and
my friend called a general practitioner
who was and is also a friend, and together
they drove over the Bay Bridge at record
speeds and somehow
settled the argument
in my favor.

But I've been using the term "mastectomy," and probably that
is not correct.
I think it was a partial something or other mastectomy, to be
more precise.
And probably my account of what happened is not correct, in
other particulars, as well.

I am not a nurse. I am not a doctor.

I have a really poor memory of what happened to me, after my friend, Dr. Allen Steinbach, said, "There's bad news."

But I have my body and
I have my right hand at the end of my right arm
that I couldn't use or move for months.
And none of that distorts or hallucinates or exaggerates.

Whatever kind of mastectomy was done to me means that I have what looks like a poorly executed stitch situation where other women have flesh and skin and contour.

I have scar tissue and discoloration.
I have no nipple.
I have no nerve endings.
I have no sensations whatsoever.
I have a permanent wound site that I detest.
To this moment,
it infuriates me to see this mutilation.
I have heard about and seen other women who
take photographs of themselves, naked,
after mastectomies.
I have heard about and seen other
women who avail themselves of
cosmetic efforts such as padded bras
or tattoo simulation of a nipple, and
so on and so on

And I admire and applaud each and every woman who devises some way to survive breast cancer any way she can.

But the fact is that after agreeing to the mutilation of a mastectomy because I thought that that surgery would extirpate the disease from my life and assure my estimated 80 percent chance of survival

the fact is that, after that mutilation took place on my own
  body,
I had to sit and listen to the further what-you-might-call-Bad-
  News
that now my chances of survival had been reevaluated at 40
  percent.
And I felt furious then. And I feel furious now.
And I felt helpless then.
And I feel helpless now.

And from that consultation forward I have been living with A
Worst Case Scenario of a 40 percent prognosis for survival and, well,
this is all integral to The Breast Cancer Mystery and Horror that
nobody knows how to interrupt.
  And that totally pisses me off.

I mean, living with a 40 percent prognosis
is really quite weird.
Between that and living
with a grotesque stitch instead of a breast
I'd have to admit
I can't make a choice: Both conditions make you crazy.
  It means you are terrified of love.
  It means you never want to undress in front of anybody.
  It means all references to future time
  frighten you or leave you feeling
  ignored or irrelevant or both.
  It means no long-range plans.
  It means that anytime anything slightly unusual
  comes up, physically, your doctors fly
  into first gear with blood tests and
  scans and mammograms and biopsies.
  It means that doctors go into first gear three or four times a
    year.

It means you represent an unbearable
emotional rollercoaster to your family and friends.

It means that you can't figure out
whether you should feel like
a winner or a loser.

It means death is always always
blurring your vision with tears.

It means that everytime the tests
come back negative you feel like
you don't want to imagine
what will happen if and when
they don't. And you feel
there is an inevitability
about this whole torturous
process that is not
necessarily going to end
happily.
And because
your family and your friends
weep and hug you and
express so much relief and love
each time the repeated ordeal
of these tests concludes,
you feel like you want to be
a winner. You really do.
But you don't know how

Nobody knows.
And that totally pisses me off.
I live here in the Bay Area, in Berkeley. The San Francisco Bay
Area of California has the highest incidence of breast cancer in the
country. As a matter of fact, the incidence of breast cancer in the Bay
Area is the "highest in the world for white women and 50 percent

higher than in most European countries and five times higher than in Japan. Black women in the Bay Area have rates about 25 percent lower than whites."*

Why is any of this true?
Nobody knows.
What can be done to end this
ultimate
soft-spoken emergency?

Well, on a personal level I am trying to best a worst case
    scenario.
I want to win this one.
I went through physical therapy and I have regained the use
    of my arm and my hand.
I am able, now, to function as a writer and a poet.
I work out at the gym 3X a week.
I play tennis 3X a week.
I eat hardly any fat, at all
I meditate
I do everything I possibly can every day.
I postpone nothing.
I no longer procrastinate.
I give whatever I undertake all that I've got
I pay closer and closer attention to incredible,
surrounding reasons for celebration and faith
I watch for good news.
I work with folks to create good news.
I become hourly more aware
of the privileges conveyed by my human life
I am astonished by the beauty and the strength
and the love of my son and my many, many friends,
I am blessed by my students at U.C.–Berkeley
who never let me forget

* Greater Bay Area Cancer Registry Report, published by Northern California Cancer Center, 1994, Vol. 5, #1.

The probability of surprise
and
The gorgeous potential of
amazing intelligence joined with
amazing positive energy

With a worst case scenario
with a 40 percent chance of survival prognosis
I am living a happy life
a blessed life

> I am heartened because I am hopeful, now.
> I am thinking well, maybe, at last,
> the word's out about
> the ultimate soft-spoken emergency
> maybe now
> somebody knows
> maybe somebody will stop the mystery/stop
> the suffering
> that kills 46,000 mothers and sisters and daughters every
> year
> *maybe somebody*
> *will save my life*
> *for example*
> and tear up the worst case scenario
> I've been living with

I mean I'm ready for that
I mean, like, why not?
I'm ready

ON THE POLITICS

OF CHANGE

>€

Keynote for the Tenth Anniversary National Black Lesbian and Gay Conference, 1997.

I'M PROUD that this, the tenth year's, National Black Gay and Lesbian Annual Conference begins on Valentine's Day.

Our beleaguered history, as Blackfolks, here, means that romance has sometimes seemed impossible/irrelevant or a footnote to lighten up a terrifying text.

I remember when one of our civil rights leaders, a Black man I adored and admired with the total intensity of a schoolgirl, I remember the first time I decided he was lying to me.

There was an emergency in Englewood, New Jersey. Not only was school desegregation not taking place, but the white citizenry there had added on violence to their resistance. Now, Black parents were furious and wanting to retaliate, all for the sake of a reasonable upgrade in the quality of education available for their kids.

My hero/lover drove us into that inflamed community. I'd never seen him lead, so to speak, before that afternoon. And I was quite entirely shocked by the force and the beauty of the way he took charge. By the time we left, several hours later, his brilliant, and summoning, oratory had convinced those parents that they should not quit, that they would not lose, and that they should, in fact, escalate, and diversify, their pressures for change—in ways he, most persuasively, spelled out.

And I thought, *This is the way heroes make history.*

On the way back I sat beside my hero/lover, speechless, and thrilled.

But when we finally reached my housing project's apartment, later that night, he lied to me.

He took me into his arms and said, "At last! I've been waiting for this all day long!"

And I thought, *This is the way heroes make out!*

I knew he was lying because I'd been there. I'd seen him. I'd listened to him. And the passion of his focus and his flourish inside that scary crisis, well, that passion was the opposite of Mickey Mouse or anything you get through just so you can get on with the real/some other deal.

He had been luminous and irresistible and 150 percent right there, giving everything he could because those children and those issues and that trust of that community mattered to him at least, I'd say, at least as much as his girlfriend of the moment—namely, me.

And I knew that. And I thought that was all logical and righteous and I didn't have any problems about romance at the end of that day but I did think it was weird, and unfortunate, and, you know, wrong, that he thought he needed to, like, settle a conflict between our personal love and political struggles. It was strange that he assumed there was a conflict. I didn't see that. I didn't feel that.

As a matter of fact, the only reason I was traveling around with that particular hero, in the first place, was because I had heard exciting accounts of his political activities and commitment, and I had concluded, "He sure sounds like a straight-up warrior, on my side!"

So that awkward moment of that evening has stayed with me, troubling my mind.

He was my introduction to the idea that you have sex, love, or both, on the one hand, and you have politics or principles on the other.

It felt peculiar, and puzzling to me, way back then.

It feels like that—badly confused, or worse, today.

So I'm proud and I'm happy that, on this occasion, at any rate, the two spheres of passionate concern fuse, or can be pursued into an equitable coexistence in which the one nourishes the other and the other then flourishes.

Maybe it's our history.

Maybe it's this Judeo-Christian culture that dichotomizes the whole world into up or down and in or out and personal or public and can't seem to handle any kind of coexistence, for example, male and female or Black and white or gay and straight without imposing self-fulfilling suppositions about conflict and heirarchy. I mean, maybe sexy needs to be redefined.

At any rate, Happy Valentine's Day!

We're here. And if our romance has been stolen or furtive or so-called "after hours," for whatever bunch of reasons, evidently, some pretty big part of that happiness got through, nonetheless: We're here! Black and gay or lesbian, or bisexual—no part of that list was ever supposed to exist, let alone worry about romance.

In any case, you know I know that worry doesn't do a thing to boost the Valentine energies in our universe!

Mostly, it's a matter of great good luck, or inexplicable, heart-beat grace.

About ten years after my hero episode, a young Black woman just up from Hazlehurst, Mississippi, moved to Harlem. She was to become my partner for several, unforgettable years. But the way we met was, you might definitely say, political.

"Black Is Beautiful" had replaced "Black Power" as the motivating concept of the day, and I'd been uneasy about it: What did it mean, really? And would "Black Is Beautiful" produce, for example, more Black college graduates, or better inner-city housing? To me, it was a political slogan that might not yield any on-the-ground change. I was not convinced that a psychological shift would, necessarily, impact upon discrimination on the job, and so forth.

Anyhow, there was this young newcomer up south from Delta territory. And when she learned I was about to visit her home base on a *New York Times* assignment, she offered to give me an annotated list of contacts and family members. She also offered me dinner.

And when I arrived at her place, that winter evening, I swear my head was full of statistics about Mississippi's hunger counties and white violence and rural Black mechanisms of defense.

But at the very second when she had pulled the broiler tray out from the stove and was testing the steak—that fabulous steak for our dinner—and she glanced up at me, well, I got it! I had this revelation. Truly, it was like a visitation of the divine! I got a glimpse of her face under that huge Afro crown she was wearing and there was nothing I did not understand.

As a matter of fact, not only was "Black Is Beautiful" obvious to me, to a most personally inspiring degree, but, also, "Black Is Beautiful" galvanized my political determinations to make all of Mississippi into a safe and gracious Black home for Blackfolks.

There was no conflict between the political and the personal chambers of my political and personal heart.

And when she went on to become, actually, the most popular pin-up for "Black Is Beautiful" posters and calendars, as she did, I no longer worried about personal cause and political effect. If you, whoever, didn't get it, that was okay.

I did.

I was running with it.

S O , I W A N T E D to say to you, let's suppose we know who we are as Black and gay or lesbian or bisexual.

And, then, what about that? How does any facet of your or my identity intersect, for instance, with the fact that the average grade level for Black elementary and junior high school children happens to be *D+*? That's the situation in *Oakland, California*. What about that?

Does our sexual or racial identity compel an activist intersection with such a horrifying status quo, or not?

Is it sexual or racial identity that will catapult each of us into creative agency for social change?

I would say I hope so, but also, I do not believe that who you are guarantees anything important about what you will choose to mean in the context of other lives.

But perhaps the very existence of a Black Lesbian and Gay Conference implies that who we are still needs organizational support and affirmation. Perhaps we're still trying to figure out if we're on or out, at first base.

I hope we can recognize that we're on, and jump forward from there!

In San Francisco, there's a progressive benefit policy for same sex domestic partners that stands mainly as a challenging model that other states will emulate or repudiate. And although corporations such as IBM, Disney, Levi Strauss & Co., and Apple Computers have moved swiftly to comply with this new legislation, there remain outstanding difficult tests ahead vis-à-vis United and American Airlines, two of the largest employers in the Bay Area.

That's a major advance affecting all gay or lesbian Americans, regardless of race.

And that's a major, unsettled argument about entitlement for all gay or lesbian Americans, regardless of race.

What about that? Is any of this keenly significant to you or me?

In 1992, a twenty-nine-year-old Black woman, a Black lesbian, Hattie Mae Cohens burned to death in Salem, Oregon. Apparently, young white supremacists threw a cocktail into the basement where she was living and she did not escape that terrorist attack.

Except for a nationally syndicated column by Anna Quindlen, published soon thereafter, I do not recall any national outcry, any national notice, really. And Black media failed to pick up the story, as well.

What about that?

The murder of Hattie Mae Cohens and her gay white housemate, Brian H. Mock, took place during the final weeks before Oregon's November vote on so-called Measure 9, which designated homosexuality as an aberrant, satanic, pathogenic disease threatening to infect and destroy white, Christian, heterosexist values.

Prior to that terminal violence against them, both Cohens and Mock had suffered from less extreme forms of homophobic assault.

But, anyway, she burned to death. And when I visited Salem shortly after the elections that defeated Measure 9, I discovered that Salem's firefighting headquarters garage is only two blocks away from the spot where fire incinerated her young body.

And I am still looking for some decent mobilization behind that murder, that burning of a young Black lesbian.

Is it possible that such a despicable crime against her freedom and ours shall be forgotten and accommodated to?

Just a few weeks ago, a friend of mine sent me a forwarded message about the death of Mary Ward:

"Mary Ward Dead at Age 47."

Mary Ward, a lesbian mother who made national news when she challenged a Pensacola trial judge's decision to award custody of her twelve-year-old daughter to her husband, a convicted murderer, died of a heart attack Tuesday night at her house in Pensacola.

The judge wanted that child to grow up in a "nonlesbian world" and so Pensacola circuit Judge Joseph Tarbuck had awarded the custody of that child to her father, a man previously convicted of having murdered his first wife.

Waiting for the final court decree that would determine the future of her daughter and herself, Mary Ward suffered a heart attack, and died.

She's gone.

What about that?

She was white.

What about that?

What is the moral meaning of who we are?

What do we take personally?

How do perceived issues propel or diffuse our political commitments?

I think these questions can only be answered again and again, with difficulty.

And I think that unless we submit our feelings and our social habits of response to such repeated questioning we will never overcome the paralyzing, and mistaken dichotomization of our lives: the immobilizing split focus now upon an allegedly "personal" event and then upon an allegedly "political issue."

And I wanted to tell you these stories and ask you these questions because I wanted to encourage myself, and all of you, to keep it going: this experimental, necessary reaching toward a moral grounding for our pride and joy.

And I wanted to say:

In Islam there is the concept of the Greater Jihad.

The Greater Jihad—or the Greater *Struggle*—takes place within us.

The lesser Jihad takes place between ourselves and those we regard as our outside enemies.

I wanted to say that good war has been waged against enemies of sexual freedom. Good war has been waged against enemies of the safe passage and equal liberties and entitlements of gay and lesbian and bisexual Americans.

But these wars have been waged by gay and lesbian and bisexual Americans always in coalition with all varieties of Americans committed to stone principles of freedom and equality of entitlement.

And, in fact, none of these good wars on behalf of gay and lesbian and bisexual Americans has been or can be won without coalition support from Americans who are *not* gay and *not* lesbian and *not* bisexual.

I wanted to underscore these facts:

That there is much that is encouraging out here.

The mere fact of publicly waged war for sexual freedom and equality of entitlement for gay and lesbian and bisexual Americans is *big historical news* that includes this crucial information: Folks committed to principles of freedom and principles of equality have added their weight to this seething frontier battlesite.

And these principled comrades have been and will always be indispensable to any lasting advance in the reach for expanded sexual freedom and equality of entitlement for gay and lesbian and bisexual Americans.

I wanted to say, cheers! And congratulations on the very convening of this National Conference.

I wanted to say
political unity based upon sexuality will never achieve lasting,
   profound victories related to the enlargement of freedom
   and the broadening of equality of entitlement
   unless political unity based upon sexuality will become a
   political unity based upon
principles of freedom
and
principles of equality.
Once that political unity becomes principled then it shall
   become a successful, unified summoning to other principled
   men and women who may then
choose
to coalesce
on grounds of principled commitment
to freedom and equality.
I wanted to say this means
   it's time to begin the Greater Jihad.
   It's time to self-consciously scrutinize
   ourselves
   to identify and to determine
   what exactly do we signify
   —*on principle.*
I wanted to say
   that nobody can convince me that being straight or being
   gay or lesbian necessarily implies anything whatsoever
   beyond sexual proclivities and, therefore, more, or less,
   predictable liability to harassment and discrimination.
I wanted to say
   —as long as there are gay and lesbian

men and women wannabes marching in the Marines
and bombing the shit out of Iraqi
hospitals and apartment houses,
—as long as there are gay and lesbian
right-wing Christian Fundamentalists
or Orthodox Jewish practitioner
wannabes approved by their
religious cohorts as card-carrying
self-appointed prosecutors who
investigate and evaluate the morality of the rest
of us,
—as long as there are gay and lesbian
Republicans who do not give
a damn about the institutionalized
affirmative action enjoyed by
white men for the past 400 years,
—as long as there are gay and
lesbian Republicans and Clinton
Democrats willing to knowingly assign
a million more children to lives
of hunger and destitute surroundings,
—as long as there are gay and lesbian
capitalists consecrated to
antihuman values of efficiency
and profit at the expense of
secure livelihood,
and self-respecting
wherewithal
and humane
purpose for us,
the people,
—as long as there are gay and lesbian
Americans no more interested
in justice and in the destruction
of all patterns of domination, worldwide,
than Newt Gingrich or Colin Powell,

—as long as there are gay and lesbian
Americans who view sexuality
as the first and last defining
facet of their existence and
who, therefore,
do not defend immigrants against
the savagery of xenophobic
hatred,
—as long as there are gay and lesbian
Americans who view sexuality
as the first and last defining
facet of their existence and
who therefore
will not fight for the preservation,
improvement, and democratization
of public education,

then,
   for that long,
   I am not one with you.
   You are not one with me

I wanted to say that
   my fight for sexual freedom,
   my fight for the right to hold
   my lover's hand or to kiss his or,
   more to the point,
   to kiss her
   lips
   in everyday daylight
   my personal fight is part of a principled
   fight for freedom
and, so, in my own Greater Jihad
I am struggling to make absolutely manifest
a principled commitment
to the principles of freedom
   and equality.

And I believe this is the righteous
struggling I must continue
if I hope to deserve coalitional
support for my love, my people,
my country, my world.

And I wanted to say
  that's how I see change happening:
  First and finally
  it must happen
  in my own heart and my own mind
  that I recognize my needs and my
  desires
  as needs and desires that necessarily
  connect me with more and
  more diverse, other human
  beings,
  on the grounds of a shared
  political value system;
  a shared, passionate
  perspective
  that offers beautiful benefit
  to every single one of us
  if we will only join
  together
  equally acknowledging our
  needs and desires
  as equally valid
  and then,
  together,
  commit to freedom
  and
  commit to equality
  as the fundamentals
  of a universal human rights agenda
  none of us

dares strive toward
without a whole gang
of principled comrades
hanging out
close,
solid,
clear,
invincible.

A GOOD NEWS' BLUES

⇥⇤

A JAZZ PROSE-POEM

1996

1996: from the Pacific to the Atlantic coast
of these United States
What would it mean to come
flying home?
  These strange fruit days
of legislated destitution
telecast contempt
boastful deportation
astronomical incarceration
unchecked desuetude
mean money
mean mood
bullet blood
needless
bully violence

and filth
what would it mean to come on
flying home?

(In the airport terminal a Black man
handling other people's luggage or
sweeping up the floor
In the airport terminal Black women
cleaning in the public latrines)

On the United flight whatever, I take
my seat among businessmen and the few
women traveling, as well = women looking
tired or deferential or poor
(OR) women not looking around
anymore

Next to the porthole window I sit down
and buckle up
not believing a word the flight crew
mumbles out about correct procedure
just in case disaster happens
Joke: "Emergency exits" (or)
   "Flotation cushions": Joke.
No shit: Disaster hit
a real long time ago:
   "I don't know why
   But I'm feelin' so sad
   I long to try
   Somethin' I never had"

Through my headphones Billie teaching me
The reasons for my trip
   Billie when I saw her no more than three feet
away from me in San Francisco 1954—I
think it was The hungry I—and she
strolled out of nowhere with a cigarette
between 2 fingers and a glass of I don't know

what in her other
shaky hand
and
This guy kept on playing the piano
while she sang the gut-down syllables
she wanted to sing
and I sat listening to Billie as I
watched her
for forever singing her song
as elementary
as everywhere
as my own heartbeat
and I loved her
too much to lift my eyes and see

I loved her /
  I sat listening
at this small table
full of longing full of that longing
that sound of longing
that sound of longing and flight
to a land you belong to:
                            Billie's land

Three thousand miles and 33,000 feet above
The ground and I observe
resistible terrain
varying colorations
chasms
dots of settlement
barns or houses
here and there
a river
and I cannot find
the markings for a human life
I cannot discern the gateway
to a city

The arch that rises
sheltering and splendid
  above anybody's bed
I cannot hear bells welcoming
a child into its own place
I cannot trace
The intimations of a human face
That infinite announcement
of the need for heat and space

I am lost in Billie's land

But this is a good news' blues
for one thing I'm not washing this window
I'm sitting beside this high-priced aperture
examining the view
and my driver's
white
up where the driver's supposed to drive
among all those blinking buttons
those numerical dials
and other complicated additaments
To absolutely aeronautical jive
He's driving Miss
Crazy
where she want to go
but don't know
diddley squat
or less
about how to calculate or guess
the way
to Billie's land

I figure Billie/
she would dig
this ride!

matter of fact
when the stewardess
ask me
coffee tea or something else
I'm asking back
for pig foot
and a bottle of beer

or gin

I'm letting myself in
to Billie's land

This is a good news' blues
about women and jazz
jazz
the saturation of the language of the intonation
of our music with a syncopated / roll / hold /
slide / hold / soul
of jazz

the takeoff and the landing
someplace you belong to
jazz / if you don't like my peaches
don't you shake my tree
don't keep bothering me
don't be messin up my bed
don't be messin with my head
don't be breakin down my door
don't be beatin up my pride
don't be
don't be
don't be
don't be
don't be tryin' to lock me up
don't be talkin' sweet and steal my key
If you don't like my peaches

don't you shake my tree / jazz
jazz

starting when
a woman's arms around me
yes
around you
and that lullaby
that breath
that arms around sound
that slow-it-down pacing of the day-by-day approach
to disillusionment
or death
that paradise that humming
close
enough like milk
to help you live
that whispering
that rocking rhythm
no
yes
hum
humming from the wilderness
of dreams
  start there
the woman of the jazz
that makes a good news' blues

Emma Barrett from New Orleans
born in 1898
or Billie Pierce
both piano players

illustrious /
deluxe
or
Lester "Prez" Young

cross-legged playing sax at 7
while his mother
close beside him
and his sister
both of them (his mother and his sister)
playing saxophones
or
the astonishing Lil Hardin (Armstrong)
piano player and composer
and band
leader
and arranger
and the unsung
rescue of her
other
way better known
so-called half / mista
Louis "Satchmo" Armstrong
or
what's the name of the woman
who taught
Count Basie
how to
do that Count Basie
Thing
Or
Lovie Austin
who inspired Lil Hardin
who anyway was making music
from she was two
years old
and practicing
and practicing
12 hours—day
unless somebody
  tell her stop

and eat a sandwich / Lil Hardin one
of an amazing
constellation of amazing baby girls
showing out jazz
genius
soon as they could walk
sooner than they know how to talk / Black
baby genius
jazz
from two or three or four years old
picking it up at church
taking it in
and making it up
making it work
in the bordellos
runnin errands runnin
  for the pleasure
of the houses of pleasure
  god bless the child
  that's got its own
genius
jazz
genius

genius
jazz
genius
Mary Lou Williams
genius
genius
child prodigy child
performer child
grown into a genius
jazz
keyboard artist
and composer

and arranger
reigning
brilliant from the 1920s vaudeville
circus circuits
straight through swing
through be-bop
through a later on teaming up with Cecil Taylor
through the end
of her music that does not end
through historical
remarks like this one
from historical jazz critic
Barny Ulanov
writing about Mary Lou
Williams
in 1949
"So finally has she made it
that in discussing her work
one almost forgets,
she's a woman"* / Mary Lou Williams
reigning
brilliant
in her jazz
or
remember again about
Lil Hardin Armstrong
seven weeks
after Satchmo dies
in 1971
Lil Hardin
at the age of 69
playing "When
The Saints Come
Marchin In"

* Dahl, Linda. *Stormy Weather*, p. 60.

in tribute to her
Louis Armstrong
on TV live she
was playing "When The Saints
Come Marchin
In"
for Louis Armstrong when she
Lil Hardin Armstrong
died at the piano
playing
for that man that left her
and bereft her
she
died playing the piano
or you ever hear
about Mamie Smith?
in 1920
Okeh records release
her bluesong
"Crazy Blues"
and didn't that sell
"75,000 copies
in the first month of its release
and eventually
nearly three million?!"*
Mamie Smith
in 1920
USA
you ever hear of Mamie Smith?
Or (absolutely) what about
the International Sweethearts of Rhythm—
all-girl (14 to 15 years old)
Black and Asian and White
high school students

* Dahl, Linda. *Stormy Weather,* p. 105.

crossed all kinds of borders / state lines
taking off
from Piney Woods
in Mississippi
taking on the winners' limelight at the Apollo
then Chicago
then overseas / the USO / in World War II
and then back for /
RCA Victor /
The International Sweethearts of Rhythm
a big 16-piece band
with Helen Jones
and Ira Bell Byrd on trombones
and Willie MaeLee Wong, on trumpet and violins
and Johnnie Mae Rice, piano
and Pauline Breddy, drums
when they got started / 1938
raising money
for the Piney Woods School
in Piney Woods Mississippi
who
(the original Sweethearts)
turned down
high school diplomas / so that they
could stay on the road
in a bus
with a traveling chaperone
to make sure nothing too serious got lost
among all of them
teenage musician
celebrities so decorous so invincible
in the youth
of their jazz
jazz
  This is a good news' blues
from

the sun and the moon
of Ma Rainey to Bessie Smith
to Lady Day
radiating and penetrating
consciousness
like salt
dissolve like sugar
radiate and penetrate
to consciousness
to spirit in Billie's land
  god bless the child
  that's got its own
like so many jazz
genius women
Billie
sang her way into and out of
any kind of pain
including how much she hurt so much /
her mother
when Billie asked her one night for
some money
her mother
standing in the restaurant
bought and paid for her
by Billie's love / her mother
Billie's mother that one night
told Billie no
turned Billie out
  god bless the child
  that's got its own
so Billie wrote a song
about that
and moved on
just like she allowed
herself 2 words
2 words

"Don't Explain"
when her lover
brazenly returned to her /
some other woman's lipstick
on his collar
  "Take a bath man
  Don't Explain"
In Billie's land
the blues
do not malinger
messin up your song

In Billie's land
it's never mind
about the prosecutors
and the INS
the po-lice politicians
and the sneering
and the rape
and the leering
and the rape
and never mind
Apache helicopters
carrying a war load
cost more than it cost to build
2 hospitals
4 schools
and never mind
about the elevator Muzak
noise
perversions of the syncopated
intonations of the roll / hold / slide / hold
jazz soul
  never mind
about the fist
the bloody mouth

the rape
the pretty thing beside the point assumptions
and the degradations of the syncopation
of the roll / hold / slide / hold
jazz soul /
   never mind
about invisibility
and servitude enforced
for women
everlasting
but invisible
for women
indispensable
and kept off camera
off the microphones and out the picture
never mind
about the same the same the same
invisibility
regardless where you looking
on the globe
because this is a good news' blues
Hear it?
And if you didn't know
you know
And if you never knew
you know
And if you ever forget
And if you ever forget
this is a good news' blues
from Mamie Smith
to white and Black
all-women's bands
even before the first World War arrived
this is a good news' blues
from Ella and her Tiskit and her Tasket
And her green and yellow basket

to Sarah In This World I'm Glad There Is You Vaughn
To Dinah and The Difference A Day Makes Washington
To Nina I Want A Little Sugar In My Bowl Simone
to Betty Carton
to Carmen MacCrae
to Peggy Lee
to Marion McPortland
to Melba Liston
to Fostina Dixon
to Junko Onishi
to Paula Williams
to Terry Lyne Carrington
to Vicki Randle
to Mirden Voyage
to Dive
to the almighty music of an old and new testament
our sound
our humming
our drumming
our songs of longing
and flight
to the incontestable fact
that *Madame Jazz* by Leslie Gourse
published by Oxford University Press
1995
carries an Appendix
listing
"Women Instrumentalists Active
in the 1980s and early 1990s"
in just fine n' dandy print
that list alone
is *fifty-three* pages long!
  This is a good news' blues!
Because Miss Crazy ain' no part of major craziness
about no domination
male supremacy

and every rotten every misbegotten supremacist policy /
supremacist plan
and Miss Crazy
do not tolerate
no count fools
to ignorant
to take care of business
next door
on the corner
in the kitchen
no count fools
too ignorant
to take care of business
when the lights are low
and when they blow
no count fools
  Take a bath man
  Don't Explain
no count fools
too ignorant
to hush the longing

Put that longing up against the Pentagon
the Senate
and the House of Representatives
Put that longing on a first-class
postage stamp
and tell the leaders
lick it
lick it
never kick it
  what would it mean
  to come on
  flying home
    to Billie's land
I don't know why

but I'm feeling so sad
I long to try
somethin I never had
  what would it mean
  to belong to
  someplace
  somebody
no craziness can kill or erase?
I can trace
the intimations of a human face
that infinite announcement
of the need for heat and scape

I hear that sound
I live listening to that jazz and woman
sound of longing
that jazz and woman
sound of longing and of flight
into a land you belong to
  Billie's land

(Well, I used to go crazy
just waitin' for my baby
to maybe
maybe show me
what I
needed to get by)

I'm feelin kind of upbeat / haven't slept a wink
I walk the floor I lock the door
And in-between I drink
black coffee
sweet love feel so good
sweet feel like good lovin should

I'm singin past the shadow
from one o'clock to four
And Lord how fast the hours go

And all the while I pour
black coffee

Since the blues left my sky

I'm runnin out on Monday
To chase down all my Sundays

Now a man must be pushing and shoving
But a woman's born to strut and stretch
To go outside (for / catch some) lovin
Get over past regrets
I'm liftin weights and wearin sweats
black coffee
Opens up my eye
chillin all the mornin
And thrillin through the night
And in-between in my own scene
well everything's all right
black coffee
opens up my eye

And if I want to rewrite
all the sorry-ass /
victim / passive / feminine /
traditional
propaganda
spinnin out here
    ain' nobody's business
    if I do

I been lost
but
I been found
    I am bound
    for Billie's land

that place of longing
where the angels learn

to sing and play
  the syncopated music
  of my soul

PARTIAL BIBLIOGRAPHY

Dahl, Linda. *Stormy Weather: The Music and Lives of a Century of Jazzwomen.* Pantheon Books, 1984.

Handy, D. Antoinette. *The International Sweethearts of Rhythm.* Scarecrow Press, Inc., 1983.

Lyons, Len. *The Great Jazz Pianists.* Da Capo Press, 1983.

Placksin, Sally. *Jazzwomen 1900 to the Present.* Pluto Press, 1982.

Unterbrink, Mary. *Jazz Women at the Keyboard.* McFarland, 1983.

THE REVOLUTION NOW:

UPDATE ON BELOVED

COMMUNITY

⊰⊱

Written for the January 21, 1997, celebration of the life and work of Dr. Martin Luther King, Jr., at Emory University, Atlanta, Georgia.

WHEN DR. KING published *Where Do We Go From Here—Chaos or Community,* in 1967, he was writing, as always, from a position of imperturbable faith. It is clear, reading his eloquent and reasoned arguments, today, that he understood the possibilities for worldwide cruelty and fratricide better, and more deeply, than any other statesman or CEO.

He was already alarmed about the volatile amorality of automation, cybernation, and our naive infatuation with speed and so-called efficiency.

He dissected and righteously disdained alleged Black provocations of a "white backlash." It was not that "The Negro" wanted too much too fast, Dr. King patiently explained. It was that most white Americans balked at our nonnegotiable quest for equality. The cost of providing for equality for a people denied rights of education, rights of contract, rights of due process and equal protection under the law, the cost of creating equality where, for hundreds of years we had been denied fundamental recognition as 100 percent human beings—that cost would be very big, indeed: About the same as the cost of one year's war waged against the citizens and the countryside of Vietnam.

Aiming for freedom from legalized segregation and state-sanctioned violence seemed enough, or good enough, to many of our erstwhile white comrades.

But freedom from something is not the same as equality of life, liberty, and the pursuit of happiness.

Just as the North felt satisfied to win the Civil War and "set the slaves free," the end of the sixties found hordes of our civil rights comrades fading away.

The Civil War had set us "free" to wander a racist wilderness where, forcibly illiterate and forcibly unskilled and forcibly destitute of capital or land or access to capital or land, and forcibly kept out of any promising employment apprenticeship, we were, nevertheless, expected to celebrate that peculiar ending of our enslavement and we were watched and measured and criticized and, quickly, condemned as unequal to the sons and daughters of our former slaveowners, because, given our "freedom" without equality, we could not be or become equal.

Then, in 1967, Dr. King was reflecting upon the past decade of integrating lunch counters, interstate travel, and the whole hoop-de-doo of the voter electorate, and he was saying, "Fine. But what about equality?!"

And, as he wrote back then, he did mean "equality," not improvement, not progress, but *equality*.

Equality meant that if you have a nice apartment in a nice neighborhood with reliable mail delivery and garbage collection, so do I.

Equality meant if you have a public school building that's pleasant and comfortable and if you have a public school curriculum that teaches your children about themselves and their ancestors and their distinctive culture, so do I.

Equality meant that if you can apply for a job without facing probable discrimination, then so can I.

Equality meant that if you can apply for a job because you have received appropriate training, then I shall receive equally appropriate training so that I can compete for that job, as your equal.

If I am equal then I am not special or optional or a minority or militant or correct or incorrect or problematic or second-class: I am your equal.

This is why equality became the dividing line between warriors for justice and merely liberal allies.

Equality for Blackfolks would not only cost a whole lot of money just to begin to break ground for the establishment of an eventual, level playing field, equality for Blackfolks would mean giving up the privileges of being "white."

Something real serious would have to change a little bit.

Equality for Blackfolks would require a commitment to affirmative action as the mind-set and the motivating value behind public policies and law.

Because Dr. King was a man of God, he argued for equality on a religious level, as well: Since Christianity supposes that every individual has been created in the image of God, and since Christianity supposes that every individual is, furthermore, part of God, then how shall we tolerate, or defend, inequality? How shall we do other than to pursue "absolute social justice" with reverent humility and zeal?

Inveighing against a "poverty of spirit" that could bring about a horrifying demise of civilization, Dr. King, in 1967, examined the big picture of inequality in the USA, and all over the globe.

Again and again he sought to illustrate the suicidal insanity of indifference to inequality: a situation of unequal components is an unstable situation. And when that situation is not submolecular, for example, but, rather, a situation in which one human being is kept unequal by another human being, then the instability of that relationship will not prove harmless or benign either to the victim or the perpetrator.

In his dedication to the principle of equality, Dr. King arrived at an economic analysis that necessarily included more than Black people as his subjects of concern. For one thing, most of America's poor were white, as is still the case. For another, the huge majority of all the world's men and women must struggle against hunger and a subsistence lifestyle that makes the securement of safe drinking water a major, daily achievement.

What he advocated three decades ago would seem revolutionary, and desperately pertinent, today. As usual, his ideas emanated from a mesmerizing passion for the creation of a Beloved Community, here on earth. He really believed that the alternative to equality, to democratic redistribution of wealth, to long-sighted enablement of impoverished peoples and impoverished, newly independent nation-states would be the chaos of hatred, violence, and, finally, "co-annihilation."

Certainly, Dr. King was right. But since 1967 even the meager evidence of long-sighted, human deliberation has been destroyed by ignorant addiction to sophistry by sound bite. Even the then disappearing good will toward the poor and sick has vanished in popular explosions of hideous, bully vitriol and castigation.

For example, it is no longer the elimination of poverty but the punishment and torture of the poor that preoccupies our leadership.

Or it is no longer that laid-off workers organize against management, but that management reorganizes so that workers, *per se,* become unnecessary to production.

Or, it is no longer that white America asks what is to be done "to integrate" Black people into "mainstream" society but that white America has expanded its racist perspectives to discredit or preclude all non-European immigration, all social programs indispensable to anybody not born middle-class, and all non-European languages, histories, literatures.

In short, since 1967, the prospects for community versus chaos have atrophied and withered and nobody powerful seems to care.

- From 1975 to 1993, U.S. income of the top 20 percent *increased* by 18 percent while the income of the lowest 20% *decreased* by 17%.

- By the 1990s the top 1 percent of the U.S. population held 40 percent of the total wealth.

In a *New York Times* article from April 17, 1995, "Gap in Wealth in U.S. Called Widest in the West," the contrast is drawn especially with Britain, where the top 1 percent owns only 18 percent of the national wealth. As of 1994, the top 10 percent of U.S. households owned 70 percent of the nation's wealth.

Writing on this "surge in inequality," a variety of *Times* reporters have tried to get somebody's attention. But whose?

Neither 1996 presidential candidate ever mentioned this particular "colorblind" emergency throughout the campaign.

Nor do I recall any major spokesperson for the African-American or the Latino-American or the Asian-American populations banging all over the doors and the windows of their constituents to start some trouble up, fast.

Nor do I recall any major spokesperson of any native language or of whatever hue or complexion or ethnicity seizing upon this verified "surge in inequality" as the ultimate alarm: Coalesce or perish!

Because, as Dr. King wrote in *Where Do We Go From Here,* you will not have a prayer of a chance of success at redistribution of our wealth according to democratic and humane criteria unless everyone at stake—white *and* Black *and* Latino and Asian—comes together to make that call. Not a prayer.

Nobody upfront and public, on mike and on camera, has stepped up to name the one truly colorblind dimension of our lives: indiscriminate economic jeopardy of a wildly increasing "surge in inequality" buttressed by an increasing structural insecurity as CEO's everywhere maximize profits by cybernating labor out of the game that confers real life and real death.

In part, this silence follows, I believe, from entrenched racist resistance to the principle of social equality since it first emerged in a Black and white American context. Having developed and refined a multitude of personal and institutional means to denigrate and torpedo Black aspirations to be equal, having sustained this opposition through American history, it is now awkward, at the least, for white people to ask that their own aspiration to equality should be supported now that their own necks are, finally, at risk.

But silence will not diminish this economic emergency: Embarrassment will not save anybody's job or put bread on the table or cash in the pocket of multiplying multitudes of the unemployed.

And since, without cash, you can't do anything, or go anywhere, I would change Dr. King's question, "Where Do We Go From Here?" to What's the Plan?!

In 1967, Dr. King advocated a guaranteed income hinged on the median income so that the guaranteed income would rise, automatically, proportionate to the rise of income overall.

He thought this was a pretty obvious, direct action approach to the ending of poverty, the creative maintenance of consumer capability, humane protection against market vagaries, biological risk, and the predictably pernicious fall—out from an unadulterated, legal devotion to greed.

Apart from the economic wisdom and social justice of this idea, there are a couple of other, less exalted, considerations that recommend its feasibility:

Clearly most of the beneficiaries would not be Black.

You wouldn't need to call this "welfare" anymore than corporate subsidies, bank bailouts, and mortgage interest tax deductibility suffer from such hateful designation.

It's now 1997, and thirty years after Dr. King put that proposal out here, it seems like an excellent moment to reexamine potential benefits of such a straightforward plan: Unity of peril met by targets of that jeopardy unified against it.

Nobody gives up anything for a guaranteed annual income. The rich stay rich. The middle class stabilize above ground zero anxieties. And the poor become no longer passive, no longer dependent, no longer hopeless—no longer poor!

But equality requires revolution.

Equality means acknowledgment and love of *the other,* the *Thou* in the *I* and *Thou* equation of relationship within community, relationship against chaos.

And you cannot achieve a stabilized, mutually respectful, conscientious, neither dominant nor submissive, love, without a revolution of the spirit that invented and imposed and enforced iniquities of inequality in the first place.

Is there reason for hope? Is there anywhere a trace, a phoenix of revolutionary spirit consistent with Dr. King's preaching and true to the democratic, coexistence values of Beloved Community?

I know there is.

It may be small. It may be dim. But there is a fire transfiguring the muted, the daunted spirit of people everywhere. Like the "still small voice" that came to the prophet Elijah, this is not a spectacular, televised conflagration. But the burning away of passivity and misplaced anger and self-loathing among the poor and the invisible and the inaudible and the insecure and the economically dispensable and the socially ostracized—that burning away persists like the undeniable light from the farthest stars.

I know this is happening. I am blessed by direct involvement in The Revolution: Now.

After the murder of Dr. King, I stopped using the words revolution and revolutionary.

I thought they were tired.

I thought nothing in the works merited such praise.

But one night, a few months ago, I found the revolution nailed to my front door. Pages and pages of new poetry brightened the evening darkness with their solid light. And I found them fluttering there, in slightly risen wind, as definite and as faithful as that long ago revolutionary proclamation hammered into history by the first Martin Luther. Student poet revolutionaries had written their poems for the world to read, and heed. And, assuming that I might be able to abet that ambition, they'd come to my door by foot, by bike, and by car, and then they'd left this poetry by itself, disquieting the rather cool air.

That act symbolizes the number one attribute of these new revolutionaries.

TRUST

They believe that someone will come along
and listen to what they have tried to say.

They believe that when someone comes along
and hears what they, the poets, think
desire, or despise, a trustworthy
conversation will become possible

They believe that important, truthful conversation
between people fosters and defends
the values of democratic equality

They believe that other people deserve
supreme efforts of care and honest utterance

Revolutionary trust is something I first discovered in the heart of Mississippi's Mrs. Fannie Lou Hamer, and then in the comradely practice of Nicaraguan Sandinistas, and then in the perpetual high hilarity among my friends in South Africa's ANC, and then in the upclose stories and jokes shared by IRA members and partisans of Northern Ireland.

The trust characteristic of U.C.–Berkeley's revolutionary student poets arrives from a set of related but different starting points. They have learned the necessity for trust because, as poets, they attempt to say, out loud, exactly what hurts or delights them. They reach for words that create rather than attenuate community. They witness what happens when anybody tells the truth and, therefore, they try to protect and expand the intentional safe space that telling the truth requires.

Most recently, these poets had been studying the revolutionary student poets of China's Democracy Movement. First in 1976 and then in 1989, in Tiananmen Square, a core of "misty" poets had emerged, beloved, pivotal, and variously destined for exile, imprisonment, or death. Young Chinese Revolutionary poets such as Bei Dao, Shu Ting, Gu Cheng, and Duo Duo, had risked everything to put their ideas and daydreams and faith into imagery and cadence and memorable, terse phrase, on paper. And, in so doing, and then, having done so, they put their lives at risk, as well.

They wanted to start a trustworthy conversation with their ruling elders. They wanted an end to meaningless pronouncements and the horrible consequences that follow from official corruption of all public discourse.

I will never forget that lone student of Tiananmen Square who danced his defiance of a monstrous army tank that, finally, came to a halt, rather than roll right over his courage, rather than crush his very breath.

And I had thought I might never again see anything quite so emblematic and improbable and daring and simple until U.C.–Berkeley student revolutionaries sat, talking, in the aftermath of California's majority vote for Proposition 209—which makes affirmative action illegal. They were hurt. They were shocked. They thought for sure they should figure out now a way to say "NO," a way to refuse compliance with 209. And fasting emerged as the collective tactic of choice.

One of the poets, Emily Derr, said she'd been studying Gandhi, in another class, and that "kind of a traditional fast would be when you're really disgusted, really, really pissed, because it seems like the whole world sucks, and so you just fast and fast until, well, until you die."

The ensuing silence was really difficult. I knew that "the whole world sucks" would be a not unreasonable assessment of things, given "the choice of Bill or Bob," given the popularity of Bill Clinton's war on the poor, given this latest California initiative against equality and against emerging and day-to-day justice.

The pure beauty of that moment bespoke the purity of the reasoning of these revolutionaries: If evil surrounds you and abounds, and if you eschew violence, and if you, apparently, cannot persuade a majority of folks to vote against what's wrong, then, perhaps, fasting to the death is one appropriate response.

After another minute Emily added, "That's pretty serious."

Nobody said anything. And then, another student poet, Rana

Halpern, managed, finally, to ask, "Is there a less traditional kind of fast?"

And with that, the balance of feeling in the room shifted toward tactical survival in order to continue, and even lead, the fight against what's wrong.

The next day, another of these student poet revolutionaries, Shelly Teves, brought in a two-and-a-half-page, single-spaced, typed memo, entitled, "What You Might Want To Know About Fasting" that included subheadings such as, "A Nonfiction Parable," "Knowing the Force," and "My pH is a Big Deal."

This is the revolution: Now.

These revolutionary student poets consciously placed themselves inside an evolutionary context illuminated by the Palestinian Intifada: A recurrent uprising of teenagers and children who hurl bottles and stones against an armed illegal occupying force that adheres to an official "broken bones" policy and that, most recently, has defended torture as a legitimate facet of its alleged needs for self-defense.

They place themselves inside the Chinese Students Democracy Movement that culminated in mass, resolute rebellion met by massacre and extreme, ongoing persecution.

They stand upon precepts of Islam and the world views of Buddha, Confucius, and Lao Tzu:

World views resting upon the belief that man is by nature good, that equality is a logical value given the infinite connectedness of human life, and that community is what we will perish without.

And so, assuming ignorance rather than malevolence, they resolved to educate the American Public about affirmative action:

What that means
How it works
Why it's a necessary, and even
a visionary goal for all
the people of these United States

And so they prepared to write and read their poems because revolution means telling the truth.

And so they bonded together against what's wrong *as a collective* because the collective is the beginning and the point.

These U.C.–Berkeley student revolutionaries are male, female, white, Black, biracial, Chinese, Vietnamese, Philippine, Korean, Chicano, Chicana, Native American, gay, straight, bisexual, working class, middle class, and wealthy.

These are their names: Alegría Barclay, Xochi Candelaria, Gary Chandler, Erwin Cho-Woods, Emily Derr, Jill Guerra, Rana Halpern, Dima Hilal, Aaron Jafferis, David Keiser, John Koo, Marisa Loeffen, Belinda Lyons, Maiana Minahal, Alison Peters, Laine Proctor, Marcos Ramirez, Shelly Teves, Marina Wilson.

On November 5, 1996, California voted 54 percent to 46 percent in favor of Proposition 209. On November 5, 1996, proponents of Proposition 209 declared an unmitigated victory against affirmative action, nationwide.

One week later, these student poet revolutionaries began a collective fast against 209.

They stopped eating.

They stopped everything except the commitment of their bodies and their hearts and their minds to the resurrection of Affirmative Action in America.

With banners such as "From sun up to sun down I will fast for a seat at the table."

They stood, they persevered, they said, "Good Morning, Sir!" They opened their hands, they offered their poems, they stretched out their arms, they stayed. They did not eat. They did not quit.

They embodied the revolution of the spirit that justice waits upon.

Some media came. Channel 2, Channel 4, Alternative Radio, The Daily Cal, but by noon of that first day that began on the streets at 7 A.M., I, for one, did not care about that.

Something transcendent and irreducible was happening there
   on that sidewalk
Something that could save
the soul of this country

and that probably will
if anything will

These young poet revolutionaries had created an affirmative way to
say

No
  to the stupidity
No
  to the panic
No
  to the hatred
No
  to the ignorance
No
  to the disbelief
No
  to hearts gone numb
No
  to the power that is not the power of the people

And regardless of AP/UPI/Reuters/network/cable TV or radio
  or whatever,
these revolutionary young poets were putting themselves at risk
    for rejection / ridicule
    illness
    and possible assault
because
they believe in
the necessity of affirmative action
they believe they know the truth
because they tell the truth
they believe
that they will vanquish
the chicaneries of obdurate
divisive propaganda

because they know
there is no future
without the future of their own multicultural and multiracial
 lives

These revolutionary young poets put
themselves out there
absolutely at risk
because they believed
They would not fail
They could not fail

And they did not fail
—first to keep faith with what they believe is right
—second to challenge and to change minds previously shut
 down against them
—third to embolden and inspire other students opposed to
 209
—fourth to become a verifiable addition to the widespread
 U.C. campus protests against Proposition 209
—sixth to attract continuing, nationwide, inquiries—far more
 than any of us can handle—about the collective fast, and
 about what's next
—seventh to have undertaken
this affirmative action
as a collective and
to have emerged, exhausted/sick/confused
but to have emerged
as a collective, in fact.

Anyway: As far as I can tell, these students are the new revolutionaries and this is The Revolution: Now.
And I believe Dr. King would love and embrace these new
members of Beloved Community. With all my heart, I believe he
would rejoice and rest easier knowing that these new Americans live
and work faithful to that most difficult, that most decisive value:
human equality.

I am privileged to close with the poem "Why we fast," written by the twenty-one-year-old Vietnamese-American poet Alegría Barclay:

WHY WE FAST

This is not a simple story
nothing so apparent as Black vs. white
yellow vs. Black brown vs. white
nothing that responds to their palette of hatred
this is something more terrifying and complex
We speak now in tongues of hunger and death
We speak now of our choice that is no choice
nothing so simple as I want to go hungry
but
I must go hungry
between our children and this world
lies but our own thin skin
the hollow framework of our bones
our fragile bodies interwoven
to catch the present
before it fragments into the future
This is not a simple story
We speak not only with words
but with the slender hands of sacrifice
we sign our hope for tomorrow
we speak now of respect not of rhetoric
we speak of yourselves to you America
that calls us undeserving
give us the respect you offer the stars
their distance so great
you feel safe in finding them beautiful
and though we are close to you
so close the grass whispers our names
the rain washes your hair with our voices
the wind brushes the world with our hands

so close we live in your mirrors
so close we are the pounding in your blood
give us the love you offer yourself
holding your body close as you sleep
We speak no longer of color, sex or whom we love
We speak now of humankind
We are closer to you than the ground
you walk upon
We are your skin, your teeth, your nails,
your tongue
We are the feet that carry you
the body that gives you birth
the rhythm of your heart
give us that respect
We show you our hunger
our despair
the blood beneath our words
We show you hatred
and the many shapes it takes
a bullet a bat
a burnt church a callused hand
bent back poisoned lung pink slip
broken bone
a factory a sweatshop a school
we show your no work no land
no sleep no choice
we show you all this
is not a simple story
but it is our story
yours and mine

Alegría Barclay
Berkeley
January 20, 1997

ROOT CANAL TO

THE FUTURE OF

WOMEN

⊰⊱

November 1977

POEM FOR DIANA

At least she was riding
beside
somebody going somewhere
fast
about love

THIS PAST FRIDAY I underwent my third go-round with root canal surgery: third, that is, in ten days.

That's a lot, and I have to think about it. I don't suppose anyone plans to have a root canal, any more than anyone plans to have a mastectomy. You can't schedule these catastrophes. But, the shock of these emergencies, I think, could be handled better if you knew they hovered out there as possible attacks upon your sanity and poise and if you therefore acted, as best you could, to prevent their crash arrival. As far as I can tell, that would mean changing up your value system and the reasons why you do what you do. For women like me, that's a difficult message to decode.

For example, five years ago, I got curious about breast implants: I thought maybe they'd make me more desirable, or irresistible, or, anyway, secure, in what was a consummately crazed and volatile love affair. And so I consulted a plastic surgeon who, after enumerating the obvious and not-so-obvious benefits of bigger, and uplifted, breasts, added on one prerequisite: That I secure a mammogram, first, in order to confirm that my breasts were healthy.

This lone requirement led to the discovery of breast cancer and a consequent partial mastectomy that I have, this year, finally celebrated my survival of.

Or, as my oncologist put it: "Your vanity saved your life."

So I am not about to pretend to disdain female vanity in general, or mine, in particular.

But given the rapacious extent of the cancer that was identified and tracked all the way into my lymph nodes, maybe there could have been other, earlier, reasons why I decided to have a mammogram.

If I'd ever heard about the incredibly high incidence of breast cancer among women, and/or if I had known about the even more incredibly high mortality rates among women afflicted with breast cancer, then, maybe, I would have been seeking out regular mammograms over the past fifteen or twenty years, yes, and maybe, furthermore, I would have made it my business to join women, nationwide, to eradicate that killer! (I say "maybe" because the inclinations of denial can be, sometimes, overwhelming.)

But I hadn't heard and I didn't know and so I simply thought I should try to look more appealing, you know, to somebody else, and, bam, there I was, totally surprised.

In the context of serious danger, being totally surprised is not a good idea.

Two weeks ago, I found myself inside a watered-down rerun of that scenario. I went to the dentist to have my teeth cleaned because I am in this long-distance relationship and I am determined to ferret out advantages to long-distance romance. I mean, the disadvantages are pretty clear! What's good about it?!

Well, I'd decided that, as they say in all these "other women" songs, one absolute advantage would be my never being seen unexpectedly, or in less than predetermined array, or with hair more than twenty-four hours beyond the ministrations of a beauty shop, and, for sure, I'd never ever be seen with dirty or stained teeth!

Having noted an upcoming reunion with my long-distance lover, a reunion penciled on my calendar on a date not extremely far off, I therefore went to the dentist.

Once there, the hygienist flipped into emergency mode: Apparently there was an ulcerated lesion on the roof of my mouth, for one thing, and, for another, there might be "nonvital" teeth contributing to that lesion, and so on.

Consequently, I have now submitted to two biopsies and three root canal surgeries and, would you believe, I still haven't seen that long-distance lover?

But that's fine: Once again, in a sense, you might say, I've done the right things for, well, not wrong reasons, exactly, but for reasons not altogether healthfully self-centered nor politically conscious.

But how could political consciousness lead you to the dentist?

Well, an unhealthy mouth precludes a healthy loudmouth, and we need a whole lot more healthy female loudmouths out here—and that's not about to happen if we let a bunch of "nonvital" situations take the teeth out of whatever we need and want to say.

This is not an argument against clean teeth. I'm fine with clean. But the difference between cleaning your teeth and root canal surgery is chasmic and today I'm in favor of root canals.

But let me finish this true story.

So I had the first root canal, and much pain followed. In fact, the pain became just about unendurable and, therefore, last Tuesday I was on the phone throughout the night, calling for emergency medical help, and do you know what each dentist or physician told me at 1 A.M. and at 3 A.M., and at 4 A.M.?

Each of these health-care givers told me to take Vicodin. And so I took Vicodin and I took more Vicodin and I took more Vicodin and the pain never subsided but I did verge into a serious overdosed-on-Vicodin-incompetent-and-dizzy-and-helpless condition which, fortunately, a comrade asleep way on the other side of Berkeley was willing to wake up and drive to my house to rescue me from.

As the syntax of that sentence should indicate, I'm saying Vicodin is not a great idea.

In the context of dangerous, disabling pain, drugs accomplish nothing except to further disable you. What's needed, instead, is an accurate diagnosis: What's the problem? Where is it located? And then you can extirpate the source of that pain.

I am not speaking against long-distance relationships which, if they don't kill you with frustration, then, like vanity, they may sometimes save your life. But I am speaking against long distance from self-love and long distance from political love that would mean finding out what's "nonvital" inside your mouth and anywhere else in your life and then skipping past the purely cosmetic and/or the pain-killer routines so freely available to us and struggling, instead, for personal and political root canal extirpation of what's hurting us.

I believe that most American women subsist with poisonous "nonvital" factors packed into our mouths and our days and our nights; I am certain that most American women wither and shrink and lower our voices and fold our hands and dissemble about how we feel. I know we endlessly prioritize how we look to somebody else because most of us subsist within a deadly long distance away from our pain and our desire, personal as well as political.

And because nobody likes a root canal.

So what's our problem?
According to a 1980 United Nations report on women, we constitute half of the world's population, but we put in two thirds of the world's work hours, we receive one tenth of the world's income, and we own less than one one hundredth of the world's property.

That's one description.
Here's another:
"At the age of fourteen I just remember thinking I wasn't very good at anything, that I was hopeless. I couldn't understand why I was

perhaps a nuisance to have around, which, in later years, I've perceived as being part of the (whole question of the) son. The child who died before me was a son and both (parents) were crazy to have a son and heir and there comes a third daughter. 'What a bore, we're going to have to try again.' I've recognized that now, and that's fine. I accept that."*

Both of these descriptions beg the question, "Why?!"

Why do we accept negligible income for our disproportionately hard, extended labor? Why do we accept less than negligible security of ownership in return for our invested energies that imbue ownership with value?

Or:

Why did Princess Diana accept that her parents regarded her birth as a failure/as a huge disappointment to their rightful expectations of a son?

And:

What does it mean that our worldwide status quo remains abysmally poor, abysmally hostile to improvement, and abysmally powerless to extirpate universal sources for our suffering and debasement?

What does it mean to accept the hatred that makes you hate yourself? These are diagnostic questions.

How does it happen that the least valued human being everywhere is the very same woman who cleans the house that does not belong to her and who takes care of everybody who will never think to take care of her and who worries about pleasing those who despise her very presence and who tries and tries and tries to make everything look "nice" and who tries and tries to satisfy the most wanton demands put upon her as to how she, herself, she, the least valued human being everywhere, should look inside the eyes of a mocking, cruel, exploitative, and basically indifferent beholder?

Why is this normal?

* *People*, 10/13/97, Diana, Princess of Wales, quoted in an interview

Thirty-one years ago I wrote this poem, "Okay Negroes":

> Okay "negroes"
> American Negroes
> looking for milk
> crying out loud
> in the nursery of freedomland:
> the rides are rough.
> Tell me where you got that image
> of a male white mammy.
> God is vague and he don't take no sides.
> You think clean fingernails crossed legs a smile
> shined shoes
> a crucifix around your neck
> good manners
> no more noise
> you think who's gonna give you something?
>
> Come a little closer.
> Where you from?

Thirty-one years later, I'm still asking: Where you from? You/ me/people of color/women and girls on the planet: Why do we accept a status quo that rejects our equal, our equally deserving, humanity? Are we waiting for a FedEx delivery of our salvation? And who exactly is supposed to send that Top Priority Overnight Item to the door? In an essay entitled "Slender Distinctions: A Report from Rwanda," the investigative journalist Laura Flanders reexamines the 1994 genocide that lasted three months, took the lives of a million people, and carried out the premeditated rape of up to "500,000 women and girls in less than one hundred days."

Flanders writes, "Up to the present, in Rwanda as in Bosnia, most of those genocidaires stand a pretty good chance of getting away with murder. As for getting away with mass rape—their chances are better still."

She describes her unwitting accommodation to the silence that permitted these crimes to unfold and murder or bleed and torture and violently expel or horribly jolt raped women into a "living death" because no one else—not the organized American women's national community, nor the African-American national community, nor the Clinton Administration, nor national media—did anything but fade on this enormous horror and then click off our national TV screen consciousness.

And in one of the most unforgettable passages of this report, Flanders tells us that Rwandan women who survived that genocidal campaign of mass rape have this to say:

"They wanted us to die of sadness."

AS FOR SADNESS and the future of women, let me share with you parts of this prose poem by the visionary poet Sara Miles:

THINKING ABOUT SADNESS

There are places in the desert still named Badwater: someone left her bones here, someone drank from the alkaline spring. I was thinking of sadness and water under the bridge. I was thinking of temper and grief and then there was that badwater, that sadness, running darkly down the hill: you could stop there to drink and die of it

You could die dipping your fingers into that bad water. . . .

I was thinking about walking ten paces behind the world holding the hand of sadness. I was thinking about the averted gaze. I was thinking about voices too sad to be heard. I was thinking there was bad blood bad water sad water between us and we were drinking it shrinking into it and rolling darkly away from the hill.

You could lose a temper to sadness. You could carry necessities across the desert and just lay them down. By the water. Lose a vision lose focus forget to lose temper in that shallow quicksand river, that sad thing, that restraining

down-dragging wet sad quiet thing. You could lose real
grief and not notice you were drowning . . .

I was watching wasted water run darkly down another's face. I
was thinking of tears in the sand and the fierce
companionship of thirst. There are places in the desert
named Deliverance; Good Hope: I was walking with my
eyes up holding the hand of an angry woman. I was
thinking of sadness, its bones bleached behind us; I was
walking with a speaking woman, we were walking past
silence; I was thinking about sadness, evaporation, the trail.

In another essay, this one entitled "Welfare and Work," by Frances
Fox Piven, we learn about the real-deal economics behind punishing
the poor—who are disproportionately female and disproportionately
women and children of color. Piven shreds the perversely popular
rhetoric about both welfare and work. Behind the pieties, the catch-
phrase castigations of these poorest of poor American women, Piven
finds and illuminates the economic interests served by such shame-
less cruelty and abuse:

She writes, ". . . women barred from welfare aid will compete
in a segment of the labor market which is already saturated with job
seekers, with the result that wages for those who are already earning
little will be driven down."* Overall, Piven argues "that a politically
mobilized business community is raising profits by squeezing wages,
and using its formidable influence to change public policies so as to
bolster its efforts. From this point of view, welfare cutbacks are
associated with seismic shifts in the power relations between employers and employees. Of course, they are only a component of a much
larger class strategy, a business war against labor."

I ask you to backtrack a moment and notice how "seismic" and
"large" and "class shifts" and other acts of war begin and end on the

* Citing another paper, "Cutting Wages by Cutting Welfare," written by Lawrence
Mishel and John Schmitt, Piven indicates that "wages for the bottom 30 percent of
workers will fall by 11.9 percent. In California the drop will be 17.8 percent and in
New York, 17.1 percent."

backs of women who, meanwhile, possess the meanest set of alterna-
tives to choose between: Life-destroying penury on "welfare" or life-
destroying penury on lower and lower wages for more and more
humiliating, and futile, punishing "work."

If, as Piven warns, these forced workers are not then legally
recognized as workers and, therefore, not protected by federal law,
then antiwelfare vigilantes will have created an ancillary social disgrace. As Piven explains, ". . . in the absence of these protections,
workfare means the creation of a virtually indentured labor force of
welfare recipients."

And so I ask again: How come?

When Clinton's "Welfare Reform" rose into public view, where
was the mobilized national women's community and where was the
mobilized African-American community, and the national community of Latinos, and elderly Americans, and children's rights' activists, and how come we are now only weeks away from national
implementation of The Personal Responsibility Act that will no
longer allow education and job training to count as "work" and that
will, therefore, undeniably, lock poor people into poverty—especially women and especially the nine million children dependent
upon hopelessly impoverished American women?

How come?

THERE IS a god-awful crisis on the way: Actual poor women
will soon become recklessly less able to resist the burdens of impover-
ishment, less able to overcome challenges of illness, irrelevant education, a dearth of child-care options, unemployment, and the calculated evaporation of public housing to shelter them. This crisis for
poor women in our country will erupt and worsen and accelerate
into worsening consequences for them, and for the rest of us, beginning January 1, 1998.

And, meanwhile, there was something called A Million Black
Women's March, quite recently, and as was reported, anywhere from
300,000 to one and a half million Black women converged in Philadelphia.

They said, "We are standing, we are unified," but, as far as I can tell, there was not a single solitary piece of paper circulating for signatures to demand, for example, A Government Responsibility Act to thwart the cruelty and the shamelessness of the ongoing, and intensifying, war against the poor: Not one.

Three hundred thousand–plus women standing, unified, in one place and no political purpose to that gathering, no specific outcry for rescue funds for public education and rescue for job training and retraining, and no specific petitions to drastically stiffen state and federal penalties for violence against women, even though Black women are, by far, those women most victimized by violence in our homes and on our streets: Not one petition?!

So what was the idea, really?

To look bigger than ordinary and to gain an uplift of spirit that looks "good" in photographs of that one-day event?

I think that was a waste of a fabulous opportunity for women's power: A de facto defusion of justified fury.

Black women traveled long distances hoping to find themselves intersected with other Black women hinged to some finally-spoken-out-loud purpose that would, at once, transform both the personal and the political future of their lives.

But there was no utterance of such a purpose.

And the future doesn't bode well for a second summoning of Black women who will have to puzzle through the apolitical weirdness of the first.

And in the same papers full of the news of Black women standing together under the rather odd motto of "Repentance, Resurrection, Restoration"—I mean "odd" given the verifiable history of victimization of Black women, to date—there was the story of sixteen-year-old Lo Eshe Lacy, a popular Black teenager killed in Oakland by a drive-by bullet as she sat in the back of a parked van, hanging out with friends.

Six hundred people attended the funeral services for Lo Eshe, and one of them remarked that she thought it would help "if we could let them know we love them while they are alive." By "them" she meant Black kids, and Black girls, especially.

I couldn't agree more. And I don't see how the Million Black

Women's March let Lo Eshe Lacy know anything usefully specific about Black love for Black girls because nobody at the march spoke on Black violence in Black communities—whether that violence is so-called "domestic" or whether it's omnipresent and a matter of a lousy crapshoot with your apparently incidental life at stake.

SO FAR I've been laying down examples of show or no show: No show for the neediest women and girls among us and, on the other hand, show for the sake of show, show for the sake of trying to seem unitedly harmless and more desirable: Smiling clean teeth in a mouth that aches for root canal or/and trying to look big and uplift your image when, in fact, there's an economic and a political and a cultural cancer that requires extirpating surgery if something good, something healthy, is to emerge, survive, and prosper.

IT'S REALLY HARD to accept the consequences of hatred and, also, that there is that hatred, simultaneously. So, mostly, we don't. Mostly, I think, we accept or accommodate the consequences and we deny the hatred behind them.

It's pretty difficult to come into the world as a female baby; a vulnerable creature weighing less than ten pounds and completely dependent upon grown men and grown women who will almost never run around shouting, "It's a girl! It's a girl!"

It's difficult, and I think that our understandable wish to deny the ubiquitous, institutionalized hatred arrayed against us because we are female human beings or because we are Black human beings (or because we are anybody other than Newt Gingrich or his second wife who, so far has had the good taste not to test his commitment with something as unpleasant and unsightly and unappealing as cancer)—our wish to deny the outside hatred that deforms and interdicts the otherwise freely beautiful and infinite future trajectories of our now hate-bedeviled lives, is a wish we will have to relinquish, resolutely, and then smother with our own frail breath. Or we will perish under the assault of predictable, punishing jeopardies we can not, reasonably, hope to escape.

I know this is true. I know this is very hard.

And I believe this exceedingly difficult revision of our traditional female survival strategies has become clear, strangely enough, in the life and death of Diana.

The woman for whom sixty million flowers were bought and carried and laid to rest in tribute to her own outreach to the world beyond her unearned privilege, that woman had, not so long ago, described herself as stricken by "a feeling of being no good at everything and useless and hopeless and failed in every direction."* And, even as she articulated that tangle of tormented emotions for her own deliverance, I believe that she spoke for women and girls who confront and somehow coexist with or simply seek to pacify those horrible feelings inherent to female identity.

I know that she spoke for me: "no good"/"useless"/"hopeless"/ "failed." From the moment of the news of the car crash in Paris I entered into continuing, close phone contact with two of my best friends who live in London. They are both first generation immigrants to England: Shaheen Haq from Pakistan and Pratibha Parmar from India, by way of Uganda.

Shaheen is Muslim and Pratibha is Hindi. They are Black Londoners. And, as the first days after the crash progressed, I listened to their words weighed with such a tenderness and such a welling up of sorrow and loss that I became amazed. And so were they: amazed by the passion of the connection they felt, and crying, openly, over the phone, and plotting how and where to stand to make their witness to the passing of Diana. And this is an excerpt from the letter that I sent to them, September 7, 1997:

Dearest Pratibha and Shaheen:

I watched the British coverage of the funeral procession and service for Diana, British time. So I am a bit punchy this morning, but I am glad of that minimal joining with you at this moment of grief yet to be understood, and honored.

* *New York Times,* September 1, 1997.

It seems to me that the folks captured by the TV became "whiter" and whiter, and that the folks in attendance at Westminster were, with the exception of three persons, all white, and I thought, well, that is what she was up against, really: monumental hypocrisy and monumental disregard of anyone outside the neanderthal mold of "royal" and of "English" self-imagery. We see what that colossal complacency, that depthless refusal to acknowledge anyone real, and complicated, and complicating the true picture of our common situation, here, in the world, we see what that did to "England's rose" and so, we tremble for ourselves: If she who possessed such privilege could not catapult her vision and her desires into a safe place for happiness, how then shall we carry hope for our own happiness, our own safety, in our hearts?

What is ultimately remarkable, I believe, is that we do carry that hope, and that, in fact, we, the forcibly invisible and set aside, have always been the origin as well as the objective of that saving spirit. . . . We embody the grief as well as the wish for love that could, day after day, break boundaries and rules that, as we know to the bone of our being, will, otherwise, kill us. And I write to salute you for the everlasting sweet trust of your presence on the planet.

You are anything but invisible to me. . . .

Writing from my heart I made, I think, a serious mistake. I said nothing about power.
And, alas, that is not surprising.
We, women, we know about coming together in grief
We know about coming together against loneliness
We know about coming together in love, and in acts of committed, reliable, kindness
But we, women, we still do not know about and crave and insist upon coming together in power for power;
Coming together for a specific, collective, political purpose, each and every time we convene a meeting of as

many of us as we can persuade to stand or sit together,
united:

Power for the power to recreate the world as a universal safe
house for our highest aspirations and our universally ne-
glected, or forsaken, human rights.

But, of course, there are exceptions to our general timidity,
our usual deference, or surrender, to traditions that shadow
the best implications of our female persistence:

Certainly there are women who pursue and who exercise and
who develop power in ways inspiring beyond dispute.

The Burmese Nobel Peace Prize Laureate, Aung San Suu Ky,
is one such inspiration

India's so-called "Bandit Queen," Phoolan Devi, is another.

The record-setting victory of Mary McAleese, president of Ireland, elected in 1997 with 59 percent of the vote is another.

And, closer by, if we're looking for a straight-up, unbelievably
invincible woman all about her power to live?

This, from the *San Francisco Examiner,* October 7, 1997:

Teen Prostitute Survives Brutal Hammer Attack

A teenage San Francisco prostitute is recovering from a frac-
tured skull after being beaten, bound, stuffed in a car trunk,
then thrown into the Bay, police say.

The 19-year-old woman, whose name was not released, was
in stable condition at San Francisco General Hospital Tuesday
after undergoing surgery.

Police said she probably survived because she faked death
during the ordeal.

According to police reports, the incident started Saturday
night when a man picked up the prostitute at 19th and Capp
streets and she agreed to have sex with him.

The man drove to a parking lot in the Bayview District and

demanded that she perform sex acts and that she kiss him. When she told him she didn't want to kiss him, the man became upset, grabbed her by her hair and slapped her, police reports said.

He tied her by the wrists and forced her to perform fellatio. Police said she was forced nude to the rear of the car, where the assailant took a hammer from the trunk and hit her over the head several times.

"(She) said she was so scared and thought she was going to die," a police report said. "She then said that she faked that she stopped breathing and fell to the ground."

The man put a plastic bag over her head, placed her into the trunk and drove to a car wash, where he washed his car. . . .

He drove her to the north side of Pier 9 and threw her into the water, police said. She was able to remove the plastic bag and swim to shore and, naked and bleeding from wounds to her head, got to the Embarcadero, where a passing motorist picked her up.

I feel incredibly inspired, and revved, by that anonymous teenage heroine's resistance to hatred and the mutilating violence that follows from that hatred.

I feel incredibly inspired by twenty-seven-year-old Malika Saada Saar, who graduated from Brown University, cum laude, and then graduated from Stanford University's teaching program of studies and service and then jumped into the streets around her and then founded and now directs the San Francisco Family Rights and Dignity organization because she simply couldn't believe and she simply would not accept that there was, in fact, no agency in the city of San Francisco dedicated to the assistance and empowerment of homeless-women-with-children—until she came along and invented one.

I feel incredibly inspired by Korean-American Mary Chung, not yet thirty years old, who is the founder and the president of the first ever, National Asian Women's Health Organization, which went from nothing to an annual operating budget of 1.2 million dollars in five years.

I feel incredibly inspired, and revved, by my colleague, Julianne Malveaux's September 7, 1997, column entitled, "Working Women Look to Unions for Help." Malveaux presents this startling, major information: ". . . the AFL-CIO exists as 'the nation's largest working women's organization' because it represents 5.6 million working women."

Malika Saada Saar's upstart, aggressive leadership of Family Rights and Dignity
—and 5.6 million working women primed for purposive political movement based upon union membership
and the unprecedented Asian-American health care outreach spearheaded by Mary Chung
and the relentlessly feminist, fully progressive, media investigations of Laura Flanders
and the indefatigable scholarship and theoretical advocacy of Frances Fox Piven
and the thrilling willingness of 300,000–plus Black women to gather together in one place at one time because maybe maybe maybe something worthy of their shoulder-to-shoulder faith might come of it
and in the very heartland of America:
The two million dollar new housing complex for Native peoples with AIDS
A Minneapolis miracle of architecture, social conscience, cultural integrity, and health emergency management entirely thanks to the undaunted leadership of Sharon Day, an Ojibwe Native American who means what she dreams about
The twenty-five-year-old University of Minnesota Women's Studies Department that, chaired by the exceedingly able Professor Jacquelyn Zita, has inaugurated a doctoral program

The 1997 reelection of Sharon Sayles Belton, the first African-
American Mayor of Minneapolis
—all, all, all of these living facts of ambition, dedication, and
on-your-feet possibilities for revolutionary commitment
seem to me extremely encouraging of huge hope, huge
activist solidarity, huge coalitional exploration!
But perhaps the most exemplary, the most courageous
news about the future of women appears in a *Newsday*
article:*

A 7-year-old Jamaican girl fought back tears as she testified
in Queens Criminal Court yesterday against the man she says
sexually asaulted her.

Milton Jones, 37, who is representing himself in the trial,
watched from across the courtroom as the girl testified that he
assaulted her while living with her mother.

The girl testified that Jones, who had lived with the family
for three years, sexually assaulted her on two separate occasions
between March and July, 1996.

She smiled and appeared at ease as she took the stand, but
minutes into her testimony, the girl, whose identity is being
withheld because of her age, broke down in tears.

After a short recess that allowed the girl to talk with someone the prosecutor described as a "support person," she again
took the stand and, wiping away tears, described what happened. . . .

Wearing a yellow quilted vest and a shirt that was untucked
from his pants, Jones cross-examined the girl, who appeared
composed as she again recounted what happened.

"Why would you sit here in front of God and everybody and say that my body parts touched yours?" he asked
her.

" 'Cause I know the truth," she replied.

* "Girl 7, Speaks of Sex Abuse," by Robert Ratish, *Newsday*, October 7, 1997.

She wiped away her tears.
She was no longer smiling.
She knew the truth.
She told the truth because she could not and she would not
separate the consequences of hatred from that hatred, itself
She denied nothing vital to her healthy life
At last there was no distance between
the truth that she must face
the truth that she must tell
and the truth of the lying, hideous
source for her tears
There was no long distance left.
There was only that stunning, intimate,
and, also, public and, therefore, political
confrontation between the truth of her self
and the truth of the hatred that would
otherwise
destroy her human being
And so she spoke up
And she is seven years old
And I, for one, would follow her lead.

>€

POEM FOR SOUTH AFRICAN WOMEN

Our own shadows disappear as the feet of thousands
by the tens of thousands pound the fallow land
into new dust that
rising like a marvelous pollen will be
fertile
even as the first woman whispering

imagination to the trees around her made
for righteous fruit
from such deliberate defense of life
as no other still
will claim inferior to any other safety
in the world
The whispers too they
intimate to the inmost ear of every spirit
now aroused they carousing in ferocious affirmation
of all peaceable and loving amplitude
sound a certainly unbounded heat
from a baptismal smoke where yes
there will be fire

And the babies cease alarm as mothers
raising arms
and heart high as the stars so far unseen
nevertheless hurl into the universe
a moving force
irreversible as light years
traveling to the open eye

And who will join this standing up
and the ones who stood without sweet company
will sing and sing
back into the mountains and
if necessary
even under the sea

We are the ones we have been waiting for
We are the ones we have been waiting for

November, 1997

TRIBUTE TO PAUL ROBESON

Statement on receiving The 1998 Lifetime Achievement Award presented by The Fourteenth Annual Celebration of Black Writing February 14, 1998, Philadelphia, Pennsylvania.

I AM DEEPLY HONORED by this award, this acknowledgment of my life's work. That it comes from Brother and Sister Black writers as we hold up our heads inside this strange, hostile place, absolutely fills me with pride, and courage. This award is an incredible capstone to my personal history. And on this occasion I wish to thank my mother and my father by accepting it on their behalf: Two more faithful human beings have seldom walked this earth. And I would like to acknowledge, with loving gratitude, the decades of support and counsel I have received from the Black poet E. Ethelbert Miller.

We gather here today and I stand before you at a moment of continuing risk to our collective history as a people. We, Black sons and daughters spinning out the jeopardy and the promise of the African diaspora, we know as well as any people the terrible meaning of cultural and bodily displacement: the sorrowful loss carried by such violent interruption and silence as slavery signified.

And yet we do not know. Our enslavement and the bloody, bestial transfer of our very being to this pitiless, American wilderness, our forced passage transpired with such an absolute resolve to reduce us to three fifths of anything as precious and specific as a human life, that fiendish, mass uproot of African peoples left us staggering, without most of the means to remember and to reconstruct our rich, original identities.

We could not use the various languages we possessed when we arrived. Deliberately split apart and dispersed only according to Dollar Bill, the greed-driven condition of our enslavement denied us the basic currency for our human connectedness: Our language was taken away from us. And there are few, if any, other instances in human history where such dehumanizing treatment extended even to the violent, literal silencing of millions and millions and millions of men, women, and children. And because language is the carrier of consciousness, we, thereby, lost much of our means to collective consciousness.

It was only two weeks ago, for example, that I first heard, spoken aloud, African poetry written, and recited, in Igbo. Because California is preparing to challenge bilingual education at the polls this June, I had asked my students to write a poem in their home languages: The language they learned from their mothers and their fathers.

One of my students is Nigerian. But because her parents had always wanted her to "succeed" in America, they had forbidden her to emulate their native tongue, and so, in order to do the assignment, she'd had to call her mother long distance, and ask for the words and ask for the spelling of the words for her Igbo poem dedicated to her grandfather, who is so faraway, starving to death.

And when she rose to present her home language poem to a huge conference on Bilingual Education in San Jose last Thursday, everyone hushed. Tears washed down her cheeks. And slowly, but slowly, she said aloud, in her home language, the Igbo words she had just managed to learn, in order to speak, at last, to her grandfather.

I found myself crying and I could not easily stop. I listened to the obvious music of Igbo, as she bravely presented her poem, and it hit me that, until that exact nanosecond, I had never ever heard what might very well be one of my ancestral languages, before: Never!

And the beauty of Igbo and the horror of the loss that slavery imposed upon us fused for me and I felt myself entirely over-whelmed: Only then was I able to hear and to feel a living, beautiful language that rightfully belongs to our collective consciousness.

And today I wish to remember a great human being, an exemplary Black man, a huge hero of so many gifts and accomplishments! A principled genius who belongs, tall and brave and brilliant and prophetic, to our everlasting celebration of our collective history.

Today I wish to pay tribute to an astonishing, powerful forefa-ther of all of us, an exemplary Black man, an unparalleled role model who studied, and mastered, twenty-five languages, including Chinese and Arabic, as well as East and West coast African languages.

A great human being, an exemplary Black man who graduated Phi Beta Kappa from Rutgers University, a huge hero who twice made All-America in football, and who earned fifteen Varsity letters in six or seven other sports, besides. An exemplary Black man who sang like a God and comported himself like a king.

THIS GREAT human being, this exemplary Black man, was born one hundred years ago to William Drew Robeson who, him-self, was born into American slavery.

Today I want to remember, I want to claim this son of a slave as my beloved Valentine.

I want to remember and to praise his compassion and his defi-ance and the ever enlarging scope of his moral concern. Today, as the United States insists upon punishing the Arab peoples of Iraq, I want to embrace the lucid, principled commitment of his amazing life.

I want to respect and fathom his declaration of himself as Afri-can.

I want to follow him to the workers of England, whose cause he so passionately espoused.

I want to watch him rushing again and again to the side of the miners of Wales.

I want to intervene and shield him from the atrocious insults he endured at restaurants, concert halls, hotels, and the actual and the political attempts to lynch him.

I want to join his studies of Marx and track his on-site inspection of Soviet efforts at equality for minority peoples.

I want to cheer him on as he founded, just one year after I was born, the Council on African Affairs, which, for almost twenty years, was the sole United States organization devoted to assistance of African liberation struggles.

I want to enjoy his twenty minutes of standing ovation triumphs onstage as Othello, or as himself, singing Negro Spirituals and Russian and Spanish folksongs.

I want to understand and copy his devotion to the eradication of racist everything and his rejection and exposure of economic inequities everywhere.

I need to honor his resistance to the stupidity of Harry Truman's Cold War and Joe McCarthy's un-American witch-hunt.

I want to cheer as he becomes an honorary member of the C.I.O. and the International Longshoremen's Union.

I want to shout when W.E.B. DuBois presents him with the 1952 Stalin Peace Prize.

I want to be there, yes, on my feet, yes, laughing with happiness.

I am determined to listen to his voice and to heed and to further the morality of his world view that carried him into the reverent hearts of Black people, here, and abroad: The morality of his world view that swept him and kept him inside the hearts of the peoples of Nigeria and Ghana and India and China and the German Democratic Republic and the Soviet Union and Great Britain and Harlem and Chicago and Philadelphia and Biloxi.

I am thrilled to think about the visionary, loving excellence of his life, symbolized by his painstaking fluency in twenty-five languages—a life and a fluency that ignorant, hateful, totally wrong men, here, in America, sought to cancel with one word! And that one word was "communist"!

And what would be that one word today? Welfare? Terrorist? Lesbian? Arab? Immigrant? Child? The affirmative action of this award to me galvanizes my personal history because it emboldens my own lifework.

For the sake of our future collective history I ask that we never forget this one great forefather who, regardless of his glory, never forgot to claim our suffering as his own; that son of a slave who never bowed down to tyranny; That compassionate king who went all over the world singing our own best song in solidarity with the best hopes of people everywhere longing for justice and equality and peace.

As we say where I come from:

Paul Robeson, You My Valentine!

AFFIRMATIVE ACTS:

LANGUAGE, INFORMATION,

AND POWER

>€

Whoever controls the language of information also controls just about everything
language can hope to convey, or accomplish.

1998

TANKA A LOS NIÑOS:

quiero aprender
dime dame sonidos
tus conocidos
libros y lenguas nuestras
estas son las respuestas
—*maría poblet**

IT WAS 11:30 A.M. It was difficult weather. After a week of heavy rain, the sky crashed open again and torrents of rain assaulted the earth.

* Copyright © 1998: María Poblet. Permission granted by the poet.

This melodramatic downpour drowned out speech. The windshield of my car blurred and liquefied.

I drove slowly and almost by rote. But then I saw something. On the other side of the traffic divider I thought I saw something small and dislocated and I squinted my eyes hard and still I was not sure.

What was that lying flat to the streaming, dangerous street?

It was the body of a child. He lay there faceup to the pounding rain.

Cars were coming. Rain was falling. He did not move.

But I was in the wrong lane to stop and so I began to maneuver to my right and I was about to get out of my car when another woman raced from a corner liquor store and, meaning to be helpful, she seized the child by his wrist and yanked him up and I watched him crumple back down to the ground. I watched his red T-shirt blackening with blood and rain. And the frailty of his six- or seven-year-old broken frame filled me with shame and nausea.

I'd been too slow.

This boy, the victim of a hit-and-run driver, was now the victim of a violent rescue attempt, and the victim of my inaction.

I punched in 911. The line was busy.

I looked across the twenty or thirty feet of water between me and the boy.

Surrounded by do-gooders, you could hardly see him. But the brutality of the rain kept everyone shifting about and, at last, I got one more glimpse.

He was twisting his head toward the faltering light of the heavens, oblivious, above him. And you could see the darkness of his whole mouth consuming his face with agony.

And there was no sound.

At the end of this century I am filled with shame and feelings of nausea. I am always too slow. It takes me forever to find out what's actually happening, anywhere at all. And then I'm very rarely able to react in a way that will make a difference to myself or anyone else. I am an African-American and so my taxpayer responsibilities persist without attendant benefits of adequate and accurate representation of my views and values. This is an infuriating position to occupy. But, actually, and despite the American measles of polls and surveys taken every three minutes by interviews of absolutely nobody I have ever even heard of in any neighborhood I have ever lived in, actually I am quite certain that my particular infuriating position is crowded with most of my equally infuriated and ashamed and nauseated compatriots—of every color and native language in these United States.

Perhaps I am a Socratic idealist: I believe that to know the good is to choose it.

Or I'm a beginner in Buddhist studies that suggest ignorance as a major source of suffering.

Or maybe I'm just pissed about how hard it is to acquire trustworthy information about anything I care about: Anything!

For example, I do truly think that Bill and Hillary Clinton are the only two people who should duke it out or duck on the subject of Bill's alleged or actual sexual activities. And I do truly think that the prurient and hypocritical obsession with other people's sex lives is completely pathetic, puerile, degrading, and immoral.

I'm saying it's immoral to pry and probe and torment and hypothesize and obsess obsess obsess about whether or not Jack and Jill went up the hill to fetch a pail of water, or for some other reason, because it's nobody's business besides Jack's and Jill's, or Jill's and Jill's, and because it's down and dirty to investigate rumors and allegations and posturings about sex and related matters of a strictly intimate and personal significance and, meanwhile, I cannot ascertain whether or not the President is about to bomb the men and women of Iraq again because the Republicans want him to or because, as Teddy Roosevelt once declared, "I should welcome almost any war, for I think this country needs one," or because the feeble, most favored dictatorship of Kuwait is twittering jittery or because my brother and sister Americans plain do not give a damn about 750,000 Iraqi children dead from disease and malnutrition imposed by our seven-year embargo or because the President or the Republicans are clinically incompetent to distinguish between a "pin prick" and their first-time aerial bombing of Baghdad that, hideously distinct from anything like a "pin prick," dropped more bombs against the citizens of Iraq than all the Allied bomber missions of World War II dropped, altogether, on all of their targets.

(I omit the American atom bombing of the citizens of Hiroshima and Nagasaki from that comparison.)

And because depraved media obsession with the threat or the, better yet, whiff of a sexual so-called scandal, obliterates space and energies that a responsible press corps would dedicate, instead, to Pentagon allegations and White House muscle-flex rhetoric, it is the case that we may be only days away from a second time saturation bombing of Iraq and I do not know why and I do not know what's actually the deal, here, and this is not tolerable. This phenomenon of foreign policy or waging war according to the gospel of a press release fails the information age promise that a democracy must offer to its people and, then, realize.

Supposing Saddam Hussein is really, really Not-A-Nice-Guy: Do I therefore lose the right to ask, compared to what?

Do I lose the right to know how Iraq compares to Saudi Arabia, for instance? Saudi Arabia—our main ally among Arab states—do I have a right to know how Iraq compares to our ally, Saudi Arabia, with respect to overall literacy or, say, civil liberties for women?

Where is the seven-days-a-week twenty-four-hours-a-day media investigation of the alleged necessity for our impending war against the people of Iraq?

The only bliss ignorance ever brings about is delusional or deadly.

When the American citizens of Houston, Texas, got it straight—despite mass media acrobatics intended to confuse and obscure the question—when the citizens of Houston, Texas, got it straight, when affirmative action got on the ballot as affirmative action rather than "preference," the citizens voted for affirmative action.

But the national discussion—or worse, these days it's the dialogue—on "Race" fogs the atmosphere and then evaporates, at best, or else provokes appalling, ahistorical displays of disingenuous disinformation protected by the impertinent interposition of the word *preference.*

And propagation and pivotal functions of that impertinence, that interposition of the word *preference* depended, entirely, on American media riled against affirmative action: against provisions for more equal opportunities for Americans who have been institutionally, and personally, denied equality throughout our ongoing American history.

But did the American media chasing down the hint of a kiss, or whatever, between the President and the Intern who, it should be remembered, never herself lodged a single complaint against the President, or against any hint of any glint of flirtatious interest in his presidential eyes, did the American mass media plunge into a comparable frenzy of apple-pie research and inundate the Office of Undergraduate Admissions at U.C.–Berkeley so that they could then, breathless with excitement and blushing from racial embarrassment, report the truth about affirmative action where, for more than ten years, the SAT scores and GPA numbers steadily steadily rose, across the board and, therefore, this lonely example of affirmative-action-in-practice became the number-one public university, nationwide?

No!

And so, as the President himself observed in his State of the Union address, it is the United States armed forces that stand as the one affirmative action opportunity this nation can boast about and, evidently, let be.

Well, I abhor that absurd equal opportunity for women and colored peoples to kill and be killed!

Affirmative action means life on behalf of more life.

And the opposite means inertia—which is to say acquiescence to monstrous inequalities that crush the spirit and disfigure, or destroy, the corporeal protection of that spirit.

And on another debate of national implications, again: Where can we find the information that we need?

Where was the indefatigable, just-the-facts, all the news that does not fit into an ideology poised against democratic inclusion—where was our pitbull press corps when *Time* magazine, on January 26, 1998, went ahead and published incredibly important news?

Well, yes, *Time* buried this information in its next-to-last paragraph of a piece under the bold-face headline: "No Habla Español"?!

This was news that never made it to *Good Morning America* or *Nightline*:

"Bilingual advocates point to a recent George Mason University study that examined the records of 42,000 limited English students over 13 years and concluded that those who receive solid native-language instruction eventually do better in English than those who don't."

Show me the two hundred FBI agents "fanning out" across the country to verify the findings of this study!

Where are the audio- and videotapes?! Where are the witnesses subpoenaed from the ranks of political proponents of English-only legislation and also from the files and offices of educators and schol-ars who begin their work by paying attention to the multifarious identities of students in the American classroom today?

Where is the TV and newspaper blockbuster broadcast of this study?

IN 1970 I wrote a novel, *His Own Where,* entirely in Black En-glish. I wanted to prove that this home language of most Black children compelled to attend public school, this language despised as ghetto/gutter dialect punctuated by unprintable epithets, could carry narration and dialogue describing an urban, teen romance of genu-ine pathos and hope. I wanted to prove that the verbal components of their consciousness pointed to a complexity of character and thought equal to their way-earlier Elizabethan counterparts. As part of my story, I advocated sex education and the availability of free condoms in the sixteen-year-old hero's high school. And I presented the two young lovers, Buddy and his fourteen-year-old Angela, as calmly and romantically planning to "make a baby" together.

I thought I'd get some flak about the baby.

I never expected what happened, instead: The book was banned in several cities and Black parents organized against it/me on grounds that *His Own Where* would lead Black children into educational disaster. Black English was perceived to be the trigger to failure, not the public schools where shockingly high drop-out rates and shockingly low verbal aptitude scores held, as the norm, for these kids.

And so I met with as many of these parent groups as I could.

And I reasoned with them as best I could: More than twenty-five years ago, I was arguing for bilingual education.

Given the evident failure of public schools presuming to teach Black children without enabling Black children just to read and write in their home language, why not try something different?

Why not try the acknowledgment of the language those children brought to school?

Why not recognize that it is a language different from so-called Standard English and why not insist that different does not mean inferior, or *sub*standard?

And, then, why not proceed on the basis of common sense and lead those children into the difficult tasks of writing and reading in their spoken language, their home language? And then, having helped them to manage that arduous cluster of skills, then undertake the teaching of a second language; for example, so-called Standard English?

I was, at that time, who and what I am today. A poet and a teacher fastened to language as the carrier of consciousness and as a conduit to power.

My ideas were not theoretical then, and I have no theory to offer today.

I practice teaching young people how to write. I practice and I make mistakes and I practice and I make other mistakes and I practice. I keep trying to find the ways that will work.

It's a technical problem. I do not begin by saying to myself, "Oh, these are Black children and/or these are children of immigrant families from Mexico or Vietnam and/or most of my students are 'white.'" I begin by saying to myself, "Okay. We have fifteen weeks. What's the best teaching method to adopt and pursue in the quest for verifiable, functional, and advancing, literacy for my students?"

And then the second thing that happens, is that I, the teacher, notice my students, in every particular. Who are they? What language do they know and trust?

That language, that home language, is the basis for all of their possible achievements as articulate human beings at pains to declare and assert themselves—to report themselves and their cause aright—in our huge, indifferent marketplace.

If I do not begin by honoring what they know and trust, if I discredit/reject/castigate the very words they have learned from the mouths of their mothers and their fathers, then how should I hope to persuade them of the use and the validity of an alien tongue—the tongue/the syntax/the speech patterns peculiar to those who remain deaf to any voice but their own?

This is not theory. This is a practical, practicing educational process of trial leading to convictions on which I stand.

I am not Ward Connerly, the real estate developer, or Ron Unz, the computer millionaire.

And I know next to nothing about those areas of aggrandizement except that it seems very odd to me that either of those money-riveted entrepreneurs should suddenly try to legislate into reality their totally ignorant notions about who should have what quality of education!

Whether we are looking at affirmative action or bilingual education, it is obvious that we must (and it is now dangerously late to) insist that educational policy shall be determined by those of us who dutifully undertake to practice the education of other people.

Just as all the faculty Senates of the University of California system and all nine chancellors and the official University of California student organizations voted in 1996 to retain and improve and expand affirmative action policies, just so bilingual education enjoys the trial leading to the conviction, and creative support, of the California Teachers Association and the California School Board Association!

Bilingual education advocate James Crawford has given us a heroic tall stack of trustworthy data. Author of *Bilingual Education,* as well as *Hold Your Tongue,* he compiles periodical public findings available to everyone, including ABC- and NBC-TV.

Of course, he is not a millionaire or a real estate developer. His entire career has been devoted to research, scholarship, and analysis of language and education policy in these United States.

For example, after examining California's Department of Education and the National Center for Education Statistics, he produced a chart comparing costs for different kinds of students.

And, despite Ron Unz's claim that bilingual education consumes inordinate amounts of public funds, Crawford reports that state aid to educate Limited English Proficiency students amounts to 12 percent of all state spending for all students, grades K–12.

More specifically, state aid to bilingual education amounts to 0.4 percent of the total budget while Limited English Proficiency students constitute 24.2 percent of all students.

Unz is just wrong.

Again and again, Crawford refutes English-only propaganda with fact.

In an article entitled, "Sophistry 101: Diane Ravitch on Bilingual Education," Crawford delivers statistics that compel him to summarize, as follows: "Not a single scientific study has linked bilingual education to high drop-out rates—which exceeded 50 percent for Spanish speaking students in the Southwest before 1968."

Indeed, according to the same 1997 report cited by Ravitch as grounds for her weird ravings,* Crawford finds that "the proportion of Hispanics aged 16–24 who dropped out of U.S. schools before completing the twelfth grade was 19.6 percent (vs. a national average of 12 percent)."

It may be helpful to note here that even Ronald Reagan got it— way back in 1967 when he, then Governor of California, repealed the state's ninety-five-year-old English-only mandate.

Even Ronald Reagan perceived the idiotic nature of any proposal to "teach" anybody math or history or science or literature in a language that he or she does not understand.

But it's not James Crawford in the headlines and sitting on TV panels.

* National Center for Education Statistics: 1997

It's not spokespeople for the teachers and the families at risk that we see in the news or in nationwide interviews!

And it's not The Big Bang Finding About Bilingual Education that we encounter everywhere we turn, trying to figure out what's going on!

I mean it doesn't get much bigger than this: 42,000 students tracked over thirteen years and *"those who receive solid native language instruction eventually do better in English than those who don't."*

I'm just a poet, but, with the instructive assistance of my students, I was able to locate the authors of that study, in just a couple of days: Virginia Collier and Wayne Thomas at George Mason University!

And if Congress is determined to throw our money at the prosecution of raggedy allegations and rumors, why don't we ask the Congress to balance things out and appoint an Independent People's Prosecutor who will hound-dog each of the English-only perpetrators of highly impeachable assertions that none of the trustworthy data supports?!

Forty-two thousand students! Thirteen years! And bilingual education emerges as the unassailable best bet! And, in fact, in yesterday's (March 18, 1998) *San Francisco Chronicle,* a study of San Francisco bilingual education students documented that they exceed other students in reading and math scores!

And yet! And yet! A manufactured political controversy exists. Just as a manufactured political controversy engulfed and, temporarily, at least, eclipsed the positive, unarguable facts about affirmative action, bilingual education is hurtling to a vote by a misinformed electorate.

And what's frightening, once again, is the media role in posing bilingual education as a threat to our children who need it as well as a threat to our children who, supposedly, don't.

And what's also frightening, once again, is the not very subtle racialization of the so-called issue of English-only, so that parents who should lock arms, united, now accuse, deride, and oppose each other.

How do we quickly enough correct and enlighten ourselves and public opinion?

How do we publicly put to rest virulent and unsubstantiated allegations against affirmative action and against bilingual education?

I think that, for starters, we should notice when and why huge national realities become racialized.

Established by the violent exercise of white supremacist whim and wish, this same country that, in 1790, stipulated "white" as the race identity prerequisite to citizenship, this is that same staggering aggregate that today, on national network news, and in Supreme Court rulings, and out of the mouths of preselected so-called race-dialogue participants would have us believe that, really, ours is a colorblind/open-door society, and that anyone arguing to the contrary is just some weird malcontent harboring indefensible special interests opposed to the obvious, and obviously common, good.

That is the torturous, self-deluded, and deliberately stacked, mass media context in which any of us seeking to extirpate racist cause and consequence from our national and international histories must, somehow, hold and embolden our political space.

Things have become so twisted, now: We, the ones pushed back and pushed aside must, somehow, lead public discussion beyond our bitterly beleaguered lives and point, instead, to democratic principles on which the advancing welfare of our lives depends.

We must adopt this strategy because we, the ones pushed back and pushed aside by racist cause and consequence, we know because our beleaguered lives, in fact, prove the ultimate hazards of race.

Inside a racist continuum, race, itself, becomes a hazardous, racist construction.

It's a reality that poverty does not diminish or disappear without the advent of money: money granted outright or money available through work that pays a living wage.

That's obvious.

And yet, by racializing national discussion of welfare rights, government and business leaders of our country tapped into racist sentiments and, thereby, obscured the flagrant disgrace of poverty inside the richest, most wasteful, and economically most unequal, Western democracy in the world!

It is a matter of reality that institutionalized inequality enforced for hundreds of years will not diminish or disappear without seriously long-term institutional redress of those inequalities, and their consequences.

That's obvious.

And yet, by racializing national discussion of inequality, ideologues and wannabe Big Mouths deformed our conversation and catapulted our most ignorant, bigoted assumptions into the allegedly popular will of "the people."

Extremely few Americans endorse inequality as a morally tolerable, or socially intelligent, situation. But, if an apparently Black man takes to the microphones and translates affirmative action into "preferences" for allegedly unqualified and unduly coddled other Blackfolk, then otherwise answerable questions about equality, and otherwise answerable questions about the aims and actual accomplishments of affirmative action, never get raised. They get lost.

And at this point, disgusting combinations of racial guilt and hatred revive their pernicious abilities to worsen shameful inequalities.

It's a reality that only the indigenous peoples of this continent, and the African men and women forcefully transplanted here—only they and their living descendants did not immigrate to these United States.

Everyone else got into this mix as immigrants.

And yet, by racializing immigration—which is the absolutely normal and preponderant route to residency and citizenship in this country—by racializing immigration, too many Americans have become arrogantly self-righteous, pistol-packing gatekeepers to a house that never belonged to them in the first place!

It's a reality that, in the very near future, most American children will arrive in our public schools equipped with a home language that is not English.

Sooner than fifty years from now, most American children will be non–native speakers of English and it is already true that thousands of American classrooms teem with majorities for whom English is a foreign language.

This is now. This is, obviously, a new, legitimate problem of education.

And yet, by racializing the question of how best to teach English to non–native speakers, we permit the possible travesty of a high-tech millionaire launching his political flight by proposing the language disablement of children whose names he cannot even pronounce.

Then the media bump and grind their way into our consciousness with lowest common denominator trick pronouncements that further mislead everybody so that, finally, the racial and language identities of folk who voted for Proposition 187, for example, must shock any kind of common sense.

Relatedly, the racial and language identities of folk who voted for Proposition 209 suggested mass brain damage on the way to the polls.

And the upcoming Unz Initiative, if it's carried by the voters, will, once again, signify an awful fratricide, because too many of us founder without trustworthy data in hand.

Even as we work to extirpate racism from our hearts, our heads, our neighborhoods, it is imperative that we resist and expose divisive racializing of issues that properly bear upon the safety and well-being of absolutely all of us.

But do not confuse racial or cultural integrity with manipulations of racist fear and hysteria.

Divisive racializing of issues means that you color the picture so that other people will respond to the color and forget what the picture itself depicts.

I'm saying that calculated racialization of poverty, inequality, immigration, and education colors these realities so that too many of us begin to perceive these issues as strictly equivalent to this or that race/this or that language/this or that ethnic heritage when, actually, the issue is how will we, the most heterogeneous experiment ever, how we will devise a democratic, and peaceable, means to go on, or not! And, actually, the question underlying all of that is about principles of equality, principles of justice, principles of democratic entitlement.

It would seem we'd better get busy.

And we can.

We can contact academics who work in the thick of educational research, like Wayne Thomas and Virginia Collier, and disseminate their findings, far and wide. We can call up radio and TV stations, and ask people like Jim Lehrer and Ted Koppel to let knowledgeable activists like James Crawford be heard and be seen! We can contact Radhad Ibrahim at U.C.–Berkeley's Boalt School of Law, or Professor Ron Takaki at U.C.–Berkeley's Department of Ethnic Studies, or any other scholars and organizers working on affirmative educational opportunity measures.

But, first and last, we can admit, and contemplate, all of the meanings of the language of home, and move forward from there.

Let us resolve that preservation, use, and study of our manifold home languages is a universal and an American right that no one shall denounce or denigrate with impunity.

Let us resolve that we will dedicate ourselves to the acquirement and distribution of trustworthy data on every single subject pertinent to our deepest, democratic concerns.

Let us believe that we are not a bad people but, rather, that we lack the knowledge right action requires.

I believe that we stumble among ourselves because our right to trustworthy information about each other contends, today, with an information monopoly structure opposed to the power of the many people we are.

And if you're not only "white," but also wealthy beyond variables of the market, and if you're not only "white," but also powerful beyond inevitabilities of illness and age, and if you don't speak English only and if you're, anyhow, female, then you are most of us inside and beyond these United States.

And not one of us is safe from what we do not know.

But I am optimistic because I see more and more of us pursuing overdue affirmative acts and overdue rights to the cherishing of our multiple identities that we must assert on our own terms: in our own languages.

> And I believe that if we do not divide and defer to our same
>   enemies I believe
> we will learn
> soon enough
> to make that sound in the world
> that will represent at last
> and that will relieve at last
> that otherwise helpless child lying by himself face up to the
>   rain
>
> we will learn how to mitigate the agony
> of that boy
> otherwise
> dying among strangers.

Bilingual Education and

Home Language

⊰⊱

1998

THE ENGLISH LANGUAGE is steadily declining as the native tongue of our American citizenry. Fewer and fewer American children enter compulsory public schools equipped with English-language fluency. Hence, there is now an educational crisis, nationwide, of enormous, new magnitude.

What is the best teaching method to adopt for children with different levels of fluency in one or more languages? How shall we best hope to enable all of our children to become competitively fluent in English?

These questions confront teachers whose students bring hundreds of languages, including Black English, Spanish, Hmong, Tagalog, Mandarin, Cantonese, and Igbo into American classrooms as their home languages; the verbal systems of communication they have learned from the mouths of their mothers and their fathers.

Bilingual education has proved the best method to enable our diverse student population to advance academically, master English, and retain home language skills. Simply, bilingual education respectfully acknowledges the home language of each child, teaching her to read and write first in the language she already knows, while she acquires a second language.

UPDATE ON
MARTIN LUTHER KING, JR.,
AND THE BEST OF MY HEART

※

1997

I HAVE NOT always loved Dr. King. In the sixties I could not understand his reaching beyond race to stand on principle. I could not understand, or support, his own example of "nonviolence."

There was so much I didn't know!

For instance, when Dr. King invoked "the Beloved Community" as an ideal, I thought he meant something simple-minded like the Bad Guys Stop the Bad Stuff and the Good Guys Then Forgive Them—for the sake of an okay coexistence. It took me a while to get past the "we" versus "they" way of looking at things. It took me a long time, absolutely, before I understood that "Beloved Community" means everybody is sacred. Nobody is excluded from that deliberate embrace.

But gradually, the political, daily, omnipresent success of Dr. King's leadership overcame my infantile eye-for-an-eye fantasy inclinations and a good deal of my willful ignorance as well.

I noticed that for Dr. King, "nonviolent" did not mean cowardly. I learned that the original concept of "nonviolence" comes from the Hindu practice of satyagraha, which translates as "firmness of truth," rather than yield and kneel.

And I noticed that Dr. King's commitment to equality and justice, per se, did not diminish, or confuse, my personal fight for these prerequisites to dignity and happiness. On the contrary, by enlarging his concern for Blackfolks to a concern for universal equality, Dr. King heightened the likelihood of equality in all of our lives. The more people you could hinge to the principle of equality, the more people you could rally together in that fight—on the basis of common self-interest.

I had a lot to learn!

I had opposed the U.S. war against Vietnam mainly because I opposed the draining of finite U.S. resources into weaponry and war. It was Dr. King's principled—and isolated—condemnation of that war that lifted me out of my prior, and mistaken, narrow-mindedness. Dr. King's impassioned analysis—that it was evil and racist to punish, poison, pulverize, and decimate another people, an innocent people, an Asian people of the Third World—infused a new moral level of energy into my political activity.

Dr. King budged me from the limiting perspectives of those days; as he insisted upon the sanctity of values and people I could neither see nor touch; as he taught and preached about connections that hold among suffering men and women everywhere—inside this country and throughout the world—I could not help but love him.

He pushed me to think and feel way beyond "myself."

I began to notice Americans who were neither Black nor white, nor English-speaking.

I began to notice coincidental histories among these growing American diversities.

I noticed varieties of hell on earth following from the Gospel of White Supremacy.

I noticed an unbelievable developing crisis following from the Gospel of Efficiency and Maximum Profit.

I saw how national spokesmen (Black and white alike) played

the race card in order to blame and blind different groups victimized by the same enemies of white supremacist policies and corporate determination to eliminate the labor force. ASAP.

And every year since Dr. King's assassination in 1968, every year I have seen our deepening need for A Beloved Community composed of unemployed teachers and unemployed engineers, and teenage drop-outs, and Vietnamese-Americans, and Haitian refugees, and beat-up women, and little girls thrown away by their parents, and recent and old and wannabe immigrants of every description reaching their arms around this tenuous, muscled, embittered, faltering, miserly, violent, and gorgeous, and open, and resistant, and huge nation-state that is our America. Our need for Dr. King's Beloved Community—right here—becomes with every month, with every AT&T layoff of 40,000 workers and so forth, an imperative, collective shelter we must build and defend, or else give it up; give up that strangely American pursuit of happiness and justice.

And because I am able to remember this hero of astonishing courage and visionary compassion, I do love him now. I love Dr. King.

I have come to understand how the very fact of his presence and his achievements among us means that, without him, we are not hopeless. Without him, we are not helpless. Because he consecrated his life to the principles of equality and justice, we have become, potentially, more powerful than the hatred that surrounds and seeks to divide us.

Because he showed us the value of our lives, we have become capable of saving them.

A COUPLE OF WORDS

ON BEHALF OF

SEX (ITSELF)

>€

At the end of a rough week responding to resegregation here, in California, I came
across this remarkable sentence in the New York Times *(April 3, 1998): "The basic*
problem is that everybody has sexual thoughts."

1998

THIS GRATUITOUS pronouncement jolted me back into
another, more popular reality erected by media sex police: the inexhaustible reality of sex-be-damned.

But once I grounded myself at that peephole, I remembered a
related, less visible, but equally fervid, locus of sex abolitionists.

I hadn't even suspected its existence. I'd gone to a conference
about current "liberation" struggles and, then, I'd noticed that,
when it was time for a drink (and even, possibly, a cigarette), the
men tended to the right and the women to the left of the bar.

While this sexual determinism struck me as a little bit weird, I
was completely dismayed by events of the following day.

A rather good-looking (if I may say so) Black scholar of substantial academic standing held forth on the exploitation of Black men
and Black women in American cinema. Equipped with a host of film
clips, and super-relentlessly polysyllabic commentary, this eminent

Brother inveighed against the exploitative and, therefore, demeaning film presentation of physically attractive Black men or Black women, for almost an hour.

From the back row of the auditorium, I had a really hard time detecting the exploitation thing. What I could see, easily, were fully clothed, gorgeous Black men, or Black women, in various close-ups of irresistibly physical information.

That's what I saw.

What I heard was "commodification" and "racist appropriation" and "trivialization," and so on, and I just wished I could turn off the sound.

But I couldn't do that.

However, that speaker was followed by a second, extremely good-looking (again, if I may say so) Black man who, before presenting his conference paper on something about prisons and the sixties, stunned that august assembly of self-declared radicals:

He said:

"In all honesty, I have to admit that, while I understand where my Brother was coming from, I also found those Black women attractive; I also got turned on!"

At this point, a Black woman in her twenties, a young scholar who had earlier made quite an impression as her well-trained mind raced into and out of ideas she handled with striking sophistication—that young scholar yelled, aloud, from her front row seat: "I can't believe you said that! You make me sick!"

And, judging from the murmured support elicited by her outburst, she spoke for many, if not most, of the other young Black women, there.

I could not believe what was happening. What exactly made her sick? That this guy copped to finding, let's say, Pam Grier, attractive?

Damn! I find Pam Grier attractive!

Later on, I asked the young Black scholar if she'd been serious. And, after righteously squaring her shoulders, she rebuked me: "June Jordan! Are you serious?"

I knew I'd better believe what was happening.

At that particular conference, sex would not make the liberation struggle list.

Sex was no longer okay.

Well, behind that realization, I went into postmenopausal shock. I'd been misled. All the discussion of heterosexuality and bisexuality and gay and lesbian sexuality, all of that was not about sex! All of that was about issues requiring analysis of hegemonic consciousness and capitalistic patterns of primary affectional engagement. And, meanwhile, sex, itself, had fallen out of favor!

And just when I, for example, was getting interested. I mean, not only the politics and/or the psychology and/or the economics of sex, but, you know, the activating energies as well as the energetic activities of sex had just begun to dominate my imagination, and my daily circumlocutions, indoors and out!

Now the whole thing's gone bust.

Now it seems like nobody can tell the difference between sexual harassment and consensual obsession, or even perceptible flirtation.

Folks conflate sexual assault with whatever could lead one of President Clinton's most graphic accusers to describe herself, long after the alleged assault, as his "Number One Fan."

AND THEN THERE'S monogamy run wild: Everybody from teenagers to gay men espouses (I think that's the verb) monogamy as a realistic whatchamacallit.

And, meanwhile, a beautiful woman or a beautiful man in any visual documentation is, thereby, degraded, and acknowledgment of this or that movie star as physically exciting strongly suggests corrupt, anticommunity values.

At the least, this should make dating more difficult.

I suppose many people will give it up, entirely, and, instead, join the nearest political movement promising redirection of all sexual impulse into exhausting design and distribution of strictly cerebral flyers, citywide.

Uh-huh: As though political commitment minus passionate efflorescence of the most literal and provocative sort is desirable, or even a possibility!

On campus, correct modes of comradely interaction preclude observations of Valentine's Day, which tends to reinforce unbalanced power relationships anyway warped by commercialization.

One of my undergraduates has announced that she regards men's nipples as "appendages" and can neither understand why men have them nor why anyone might find men's nipples, so to speak, worthy of retention.

Women students summarily describe women's breasts as "a nuisance"/"a burden"/"occasionally functional in maternal situations," and that's that.

Nobody writes love poetry anymore.

"What," I've been asked, quite recently, "is the purpose of a love poem?"

And, at any rate, it is apparently infuriating if somebody thinks you're "cute."

Plus, there's a serious dis of the movie *Jackie Brown* making the rounds: When the bailbondsman goes to the jail and waits, just beyond the gates, to greet the prisoner (Pam Grier), he evidently falls in love with her: Just watching her walk toward him, his heart skips into an entire song by Bloodstone, as a matter of fact.

Criticism: "He didn't even know her! Why would he feel that way?"

Meanwhile, humorless pulp fictions become the top story of each and every hour carrying the President of the United States into a neo-Puritanical orgy of envious, titillated condemnation unrelieved, it appears, by anybody's enjoyment of anything beyond the prospect of perpetual press punishment of the allegation of sexual interaction between live grown-ups, off-screen.

I have to say, it's too bad about sex biting the dust, and nothing else.

Sex used to happen, a lot.

And some of the poetry that came out of it was pretty good stuff.

Oh, well.

I'm with Emma Goldman: If you can't dance, it's not my kind of revolution.

BREAK THE LAW!

⊰⊱

SHORTLY AFTER federal desegregation of public facilities, and interstate travel, I went to Mississippi on assignment for the *New York Times*. I stayed in an upscale hotel in the downtown district of Jackson, and I remember it was really hot. If you stepped outside for more than ten minutes, you'd eagerly trade your camera and your rental car for a piece of soap and a long cold shower. So, one afternoon, I thought I'd take a quick swim in the pool.

I switched to my bathing suit, grabbed a towel, and flip-flopped down the hall. But when I reached the pool area, a shivering of fear goose-bumped all over my skin. There was no one there. It was very dark. You could barely see the water or its concrete boundaries.

Inside my mouth tasted like blood. And I stood, shivering, for several minutes. I was afraid to move. What was going to happen to me?

I had forgotten. Or I had never understood: The hotel had been forced to desegregate, which meant the hotel had been forced to allow me to swim in that pool. And, in response, the hotel was daring me to go ahead: Get into that murky taboo cistern absolutely shunned, now, by white people.

They would boycott, they would forfeit, the summertime relief of swimming rather than mingle their white bodies in the same element that held my own.

Until I stood in that unnatural dark of that unnatural stillness by that pool, I had never felt white hatred so close, and everywhere, around me. Now I did. Now I knew.

This was not an attitude or a preference. This was shotgun-serious loathing of me and my kind.

The answer to that shotgun was the law.

You didn't have to like it. You didn't have to love me. But you did have to obey the law and let me swim.

Without the law on my side, I damn straight could not have traveled from New York to Mississippi without horrible damage to my bladder, extreme dehydration, and a variety of humiliating messages imprinted on my soul. Without the law on my side, and after so long, I damn straight could not have stayed in a downtown Jackson hotel/motel or rented a car at the airport, or ordered a cup of coffee, anywhere, or exhibited the idiotic temerity of daring to think about doing anything anywhere that didn't say, COLORED.

That's the before and after story of the shotgun and the law. That's the before and after story of white hatred of Black folks. Before, they just hated us. After, they hated us or they didn't hate us, but we were moving, now, moving lawfully, see, into the same element that upheld their privileged white bodies. The same water and the same air and, sooner or later, the same classroom, and the same apartment building, and the same workplace, because we didn't have some kind of a dream about any of these things: We had the law equalizing our rights as American citizens.

· · ·

AFFIRMATIVE ACTION is a federal policy carrying the weight of law. Its purpose is the same as the desegregation of that Mississippi swimming pool: to equalize our rights as American citizens.

Affirmative action policies acknowledge that citizen equality has been denied to us, and will be denied to us, absent federal intervention.

California's 1994 Proposition 209 eviscerated affirmative action. With its passage, it became the law that racial and/or ethnic identity could not be taken into account in matters of employment or education.

On a colorblind basis, we would now see who was really "qualified" or not.

On March 30, 1998, the Chancellor of U.C.–Berkeley convened a press conference to announce the consequences of Proposition 209. He was going to tell everybody the new numbers that compare the 1998 freshman class to the entering class of 1997. And he did.

And here they are:

1. A decline of 64.3 percent of African-Americans, who will, at most, represent 2.4 percent of the "total pool of admitted students."
   The total pool is 7,868
2. A decline of 56.3 percent for Chicanos, who will, at most, represent 5.5 percent of the total incoming freshman class.
   I say, "at most," because the usual fallout is two thirds of those invited to enroll.
3. A decline of 58.9 percent for Native Americans, who will, at most, represent 0.3 percent of the total incoming freshman class.
4. A decline from 23.1 percent to 10.4 percent for Native American, African-American, Chicano, and Latino students who will arrive, next September—assuming a 100 percent acceptance rate for all of those admitted.

   During the question-and-answer period that followed the

administration's official presentation, the chancellor stunned the room by announcing an additional fact:

More than 800 minority students with a 4.0 grade point average as well as 1200 SAT scores had been "turned away."

Some twenty-four hours later, Bob Laird, Director of Undergraduate Admissions, elaborated, with even more startling figures:

More than 1300 minority students with grade point averages above 4.0 had also been "turned away."

If you squeeze all of these numbers into anything at all coherent, this is what comes clear:

Proposition 209 is the law.

Abiding by that law, the University of California has chosen a freshman class that effectively resegregates higher education.

This resegregation furthermore excludes 2,100 so-called minority students with straight-A, or better, records of academic achievement.

Given the Chancellor's publicly avowed commitment to intellectual excellence and democratic diversity, and given the democratic mandate of public education, this is not, on any terms, a defensible situation.

He has, we have, but one option: Break the law!

It was once against the law for Blackfolks to read and write.

It was once against the law for Blackfolks to marry each other.

It was once against the law for Blackfolks to vote.

It was once against the law for Blackfolks to swim in indoor, or outdoor, public waters.

We had to break those laws or agree to the slaveholder's image of us: three fifths of a human being.

When the law is wrong, when the law produces and enjoins manifest and undue injury to a people, when the law punishes one people and privileges another, it is our moral obligation to break the law!

The law is not God-given!

2,100 minority students with straight-A, or better, grade point averages denied admission to U.C.–Berkeley?!

To the Chancellors of the entire University of California system I say: Break the law!

We, the people, we'll take it from there.

April 7, 1998
1:05 A.M.
Berkeley, California

ABOUT THE AUTHOR

JUNE JORDAN is Professor of African-American Studies at the University of California, Berkeley, where she also directs the Poetry for the People program. She is best known for her books *Things That I Do in the Dark, Civil Wars, Technical Difficulties,* and *Haruko/Love Poetry.* She lives in Berkeley, California, and is at work on a memoir about her childhood.

Praise for
JUNE JORDAN

"June Jordan is our premiere black woman essayist."
—TONI MORRISON

"June Jordan's work, at this point and for many years now, is perfect…She says exactly what she means to say, and says it…powerfully…She manages to tap that place where race and sexuality, class and justice, gender and memory come together. She doesn't go with the cutting-edge idea but reaches for that difficult terrain where others may fear to tread." —AMERICAN BOOK REVIEW

"Always urgent, inspiring, and demanding, Jordan's work has left its indelible mark everywhere from *Essence* to *The Norton Anthology of Poetry*, and from theater stages to the floors of the United Nations and the United States Congress." —BOMB MAGAZINE

US $12.95 / $17.95 CAN
ISBN 0-385-49225-1

51295

9 780385 492256